Ten Dates
Every Catholic
Should Know

Diane Moczar

Ten Dates Every Catholic Should Know

The Divine Surprises and Chastisements
That Shaped the Church
and Changed the World

SOPHIA INSTITUTE PRESS®
Manchester, New Hampshire

Sophia Institute Press®
Box 5284, Manchester, NH 03108
1-800-888-9344
www.sophiainstitute.com

Library of Congress Cataloging-in-Publication Data

Moczar, Diane.
Ten dates every Catholic should know : the divine surprises and
chastisements that shaped the church and changed the world /
Diane Moczar.
     p. cm.
ISBN 1-933184-15-9 (pbk. : alk. paper)
1.   Catholic Church — History. I. Title.

BX945.3.M63 2006
282.09 — dc22   2005033225

08 09 10 9 8 7 6 5 4 3

Pour l'abbé Georges de Nantes,
mon père spirituel et maître à penser,
dont j'ai essayé de suivre,
de loin il est vrai,
la méthode historique "volontaire."

Je voudrais aussi remercier les frères et soeurs
de ses communautés pour leurs
merveilleux travaux historiques,
dont j'ai énormément profité.

Contents

⌒

Introduction

In 1943 a children's book appeared called *Pegs of History: A Picture Book of World Dates*. It was published back in those dark ages when dates were thought important, and included some twenty events, each briefly described, dated, and illustrated with an attractive picture. The point of the book was expressed in its title: a peg is something you hang things on; similarly, a date in history is an organizing principle for the memory, a fixed point around which important people and developments can cluster in our mind. A handful of dates can serve as the structure for a broad overview of Catholic history, from the Roman period to the twentieth century, and that is what this book aims to provide.

We would all agree, I think, that every Catholic should know something of the Catholic past, because that is what created the present of the Church and of Western Civilization. It is not enough to know our catechism, the lives of a few saints, and some Bible stories. What we find in the Bible, in fact, is a detailed account of how active God was in the history of the Chosen People: guiding, rewarding, and chastising them.

And yet somehow we are inclined to think that that divine presence disappeared as Christendom emerged, and we feel unable to discern the hand of God in history after apostolic times. History, then, appears as a jumble of happenings with no discernible purpose behind them.

In this book I have tried to do two things: first, present ten significant dates — some of them centered on one calendar day, others tied to a period of months or years — around which the reader can group the main themes of the history of Christendom; and second, to point out ways in which God has always been active in the world of time that he created, and to give examples of his undeniable intervention. We look first at the "divine surprise" of the Emperor Constantine's conversion and the edict he issued in 313, which dramatically changed the history of the Church (and hence the history of the West, in which Catholic civilization first developed). We end with 1917, when our Lady appeared at Fatima — the same year the Communist Revolution occurred in Russia.

Each of these dates, like all the other dates in this book, is a point of reference for a whole era. Looking backward from 313, we see the sort of world in which the early Christians lived and their struggle to survive and pass on the Faith to their children under terrible persecution; looking forward from 313, we see the Church emerging from the catacombs and beginning to create a new Catholic world, even as barbarian invasions destroy the world of Rome. Similarly, looking back from 1917, we gain a perspective on the state of the Church and the world in the preceding century, examine the many developments of the year itself, and look forward to the decades and wars that followed it.

Of course, no list of ten significant dates in history could claim to be exhaustive. The dates I have chosen are not the only possible choices, but they represent extremely handy "pegs" on which to hang the major developments of Catholic history. Moreover, in any list of major dates for both the Church and Western Civilization, most of my ten would be included due to their significance, and the events and people discussed in this book figure in any history of Christendom because of their fundamental importance for our past — and present.

Some might be surprised that most of the events I have chosen occurred prior to the sixteenth century. I am reminded of the words of Professor R. Allen Brown: "It could be argued that all that matters most in the history of Western Europe had happened by the year 1300." The reader of this work will see how true it is that the basic foundations of our civilization were laid by that year, and the Catholic principles that shaped Western society had been developed by then. Subsequent centuries built upon (or tore down) those foundations.

Does the author expect the reader to memorize all the dates, names, and events here presented, and perhaps take an exam upon finishing the book? Of course not. This is not in any way a textbook. My only hope is that the reader will find these chapters engaging, and that he will learn something from them. For students, however, especially those interested in mastering Catholic history, it would be very useful to memorize the ten pivotal years noted here, together with the main events, people, and themes associated with them.

Readers who are off the hook as far as the need to memorize goes (which is to say, most readers) will still find in this book a sense of the sweep of Catholic history: the terrible difficulties the Church faced in Roman times; the dangers it confronted in both surviving the barbarian invasions and converting the invaders; its centuries of astonishing creativity, progress, and glory; and the appearance of the modern threats of intractable heresy, Muslim attacks, revolution, and total war. They will see, too, how some historical disasters can justly be said, according to revelations from our Lord and our Lady, to have occurred due to the coldness and laxity of Catholics themselves. They were, in fact, historical divine chastisements. Not only the glories of the Catholic past, but also its most important and serious lessons, often seem in danger of being forgotten in our time. It is rewarding to do our bit in keeping them alive.

Ten Dates
Every Catholic
Should Know

313 AD

The Edict of Milan and
the Liberation of the Church

At the beginning of the fourth century, Catholics all over the Roman Empire were suffering the worst persecution they had ever experienced. It was unleashed by the Emperor Diocletian in 303 and was unprecedented in the cruelty and variety of the public tortures it inflicted on its victims for the entertainment of masses of spectators. All Roman men, women, and children were summoned to sacrifice to the gods of Rome or die. Unlike some earlier persecutions that were localized in one or another of the provinces of the empire, this one was enforced everywhere.

Watching torture and death in the arena was nothing new to Romans. Gladiator combats and animal fights predated Christianity — part of a public policy for keeping the large urban proletariat content — and were extremely popular with the tens of thousands of spectators who filled the huge arenas. The first-century philosopher Seneca described a typical amphitheater scene:

> In the morning men are exposed to lions and bears; at noon gladiators who fight to the death are ordered out against one another, and the conqueror is detained for another slaughter. Death alone puts an end to this business. "Kill, burn,

scourge," is all they cry. "Why is he so afraid of the sword's point? Why is he so timorous to kill? Why does he not die more manfully?" They are urged on with floggings. . . . [T]hey are called upon to cut one another's throats.[1]

It was in fact Seneca's employer, the mentally unbalanced emperor Nero, who first had the idea of using Christians for such gruesome entertainments. His attempt to blame them for a fire in Rome (for which rumor held him responsible) led to his sickening garden party in the year 64: his guests strolled through his palace grounds by the light of torches set high above the paths, and every torch was a Christian. Other Christians were sewn into animal skins and left to be torn apart by hunting dogs.

A society drunk on death

That persecution went on for years, taking the lives of both St. Peter and St. Paul as well as countless other members of the Roman Christian community. Since then, there had been no time when Christians could relax their guard; times of peace could change into nightmares from one day to the next. Sometimes all it took was a few indignant idol-makers blaming Christians for a decline in business, or charges from actors furious that Christians were staying away from the obscenity and cruelty of the theaters. A riot could easily start, especially in cities crowded with idlers looking for diversion, and Christians would be the victims. A Christian could also be denounced to the authorities by resentful neighbors: maybe he refused their dinner invitations so he would not have to give the customary libation to their household gods, or he kept his children home from the pagan schools. As St. Justin Martyr put it, "The world suffers nothing from Christians but hates them because they reject its pleasures."

The Edict of Milan and the Liberation of the Church

In those days, imperial policy included ritual worship of the Roman gods and, later, participation in the cult of the emperor. The Jews were exempt from this requirement, however, and, until the time of Nero, Roman authorities were not aware that Christianity and Judaism were distinct. Once the distinction was clear, Christians were no longer exempt, and there was no escape if the state chose to prosecute them. Christians could at any time be subject to public execution: one of the acts in a matinee program for the masses.

But the masses were easily bored, and as they became desensitized to violence and death, innovative methods of torture began to be employed. By the time of Diocletian's persecution in the early fourth century, these had become so horrifying that some historians refrain from describing them in detail. They were so terrible for women, particularly in Egypt, that some Christian women were said to have committed the previously unheard-of sin of suicide rather than endure the shame and dishonor. As Henri Daniel-Rops puts it, "A whole society became drunk with sadism and torture."

Even for those who have once lived under Communist persecution — which mercifully ended after decades, not centuries — it is difficult to imagine what it was like to live anywhere in the vast Roman world from the mid-first century to the year 313. We can thus understand why early Christians looked forward to the Second Coming of our Lord with such fervent expectation, because it really seemed as if they were to be the last Christian generation. Our Lord, however, was preparing the Church not for His own return to earth, but for the coming of an unlikely liberator in the person of yet another Roman emperor.

Constantine: a "divine surprise"

In Britain, on the fringes of the Western Empire, the first English martyr gave his life in 303. St. Alban was a pagan who was converted by a priest to whom he gave refuge when the persecution of Diocletian began; he took the priest's place when the searchers came, and was beaten and beheaded. Three years later, in 306, the Roman army in Britain proclaimed as emperor a young man who would finally end the slaughter that took Alban's life. Could his blood have been the price of deliverance for his brethren?

Constantine was certainly a complex character. His father had been a co-emperor, and his mother, following her conversion, became a saint — St. Helena. Constantine himself, however, was a pagan who once claimed to have had a vision of Apollo. He was of large build, strong, capable of both cruelty and kindness, and he was certainly ambitious. We do not know how familiar he was with Christianity when he became the efficient and popular ruler of a large part of Western Europe. He did not, however — unlike most of his fellow rulers who each governed a part of the once-united Roman Empire — persecute the Christians.

Diocletian had decided that the empire was too large for any one man to control (you really need to look at a map to see how truly vast it was) and implemented a scheme to divide its rule between two emperors, each with an understudy who would, theoretically, one day succeed and not supplant him. During the chaotic period following Diocletian's retirement in 305, when Constantine would have been about twenty-five, there were several ex- or would-be emperors vying for power, and the future author of the famous edict was one of them.

Before he was proclaimed emperor, he had ridden sixteen hundred miles to escape liquidation by his enemies and still had to make good his claim to the throne. He had married Fausta, daughter of the Eastern emperor Maximian, known for continually resigning his office and then regretting it and attempting to return to power. Eventually Maximian attempted to do away with his son-in-law, but Constantine did away with him first — unless his death by hanging in his prison cell was really suicide — and then had to face Fausta's brother Maxentius and his army.

Here we come to one of the most critical moments in Constantine's career, and one of the most unforeseeable developments in all history. Before the Battle of the Milvian Bridge with Maxentius in 312, Constantine claimed to have had a supernatural vision: an image in the sky and the words "In this sign conquer." What he saw has been variously described as a cross or a *chi rho*, a Christian symbol made by combining the first two Greek letters for the name *Christus*. Whichever it was, and exactly when and where Constantine saw it, has been much debated by scholars.

The historian Eusebius claimed to have heard the story of this vision from Constantine himself shortly before he died, and there is no reason to doubt him.

In his account, Eusebius depicts his hero en route to do battle with Maxentius, who was infamous for his cruelty and oppression of the people of Rome. Then, "one afternoon, when the sun was beginning to set, he saw in the sky, above the sun, a luminous cross." That night, as Constantine slept, "Christ, the Son of God, appeared to him with the same sign that he had seen blazing in the sky and commanded him to make of it a military insignia and place it on his banners, as a pledge of victory."

When he awoke, Constantine summoned goldsmiths to make a model of the symbol, which Eusebius describes in detail. According to him, the model included a cross surmounted by a crown, within which there was a *chi rho*; thus it would seem that the emperor had seen both the cross and the monogram. According to Eusebius, "The emperor ever after wore this monogram engraved on his helmet . . . [and] he had his legions carry a standard designed on this model."

Eusebius confessed he had forgotten where the incident occurred, and some historians think that both the vision and the dream took place in Gaul, before the army's descent into Italy, rather than immediately before the battle. This is plausible because of the time it would have taken to make the model and get it reproduced on the battle gear and banners of the army. In any case, in a campaign that has been compared with Napoleon's invasion of Italy, Constantine and his army of perhaps forty thousand men proceeded through the countryside, where they were often welcomed as liberators, and finally confronted the hundred-thousand-strong force of Maxentius, along the Tiber River, less than ten miles from Rome.

Maxentius had been frantically consulting all the pagan priests and magicians he could find, to enlist the support of the gods of Rome. Certainly no strategist, he had led his army across the river from the Roman side by the only bridge in the area, the Milvian, and by a bridge of boats. He had his troops strung out with their backs to the river, so that when they broke under Constantine's charge, their retreat was doomed. Maxentius himself fell with his horse and all his armor into the river and drowned. A triumphant Constantine entered Rome on October 29, 312, and the beleaguered Christian community saw in his victory the hand of God delivering them.

If this did not make him an instant Christian, it certainly would have made him think about the religion of his mother, and disposed him to favor its practitioners. The fact that he so publicly adopted the sacred symbols of Christianity, however, would seem tantamount to a profession of faith in the Christian God. When a pagan statue was dedicated to him in Rome, he had a cross placed in its hand. This conversion of Constantine was of incalculable importance for Western history. The author of the article on the topic in the authoritative *Dictionnaire Apologétique de la Foi Catholique* writes, "It was thus a complete reversal, and history has no record of a more profound revolution."

Once Constantine had become the undisputed co-emperor, he and his partner, Licinius, had a monumental task ahead of them in restoring order and stability to the tottering Empire — a project that would now include official toleration of the growing Christian population.

The edict

Constantine did not stay long in Rome. There was much to do in the other cities of his new territory, and at the end of January 313, he left for Milan, where his sister was to be married to his co-emperor, Licinius. Milan was a strategic stronghold for monitoring affairs in both Gaul and Italy, and thus a suitable place for an extended meeting of the two rulers. What is called the Edict of Milan was probably drafted in February and March of 313. It seems it was less a formal proclamation than a protocol agreed upon by the emperors; its main features appear both in the recorded letters of the two and in the proclamation that Licinius had posted when he went to Nicomedia in June, summarizing the new policy.

According to the form in which we have it today, the document granted "free and absolute permission to practice their religion to the Christians," and to "every man . . . free opportunity to worship according to his own wish." It also ordered the restoration of confiscated Christian property, and directed that these provisions should be widely publicized.

What would Roman Christians reading this document have made of it? After nearly three centuries of harrowing persecution by the Roman state, it might have seemed too good to be true. After all, both emperors were still thought to be pagan, although there were stories about Constantine's strange experience before the Battle of the Milvian Bridge. Grants of toleration of Christians were not unknown — in fact, the same emperors had issued one just the year before — but in the past, they had always proved temporary, and the horror had always begun anew. So, along with the hope that might have welled up in the heart of Christians who read the edict, there might also have been skepticism; they would wait, warily, and see how it all turned out. For the time being, the faithful and their priests and bishop meeting in the catacombs for Mass would still be looking carefully over their shoulders to make sure they had not been followed.

As it turned out, the Edict of Milan was to be the great charter of liberation for the Catholic Church: one of those stunning divine surprises that punctuate Catholic history. Virtually everything in the lives of the Christians — at least in the West, because persecution continued for a short period in parts of Asia Minor and Egypt — was about to change.

After the edict

The immediate consequence was the permanent cessation of persecution; the temporary "toleration" of Christianity proclaimed in 312 now became a civil right. The Christian community was able at last to leave the catacombs and worship publicly in perfect safety. Already in 313 Pope Miltiades was holding a council in the former palace of Constantine's wife, Fausta, which had been given to him by the imperial family. Constantine himself (as well as his mother) built magnificent churches for Christian worship and also implemented a number of pro-Christian measures. He declared Sunday a day of rest, for example, and made laws against some of the immoral practices of that notoriously immoral society. He also forbade crucifixion; but he failed to abolish the violent spectator "entertainments" of which the citizens were so fond. Some depraved habits are not so easily suppressed, it seems. Among the people, Christian names, customs, and feasts became popular, increasing their receptivity to Christian teaching.

In 325 a glorious landmark in Church history occurred. The bishops had for years been holding councils openly, above ground, without posting sentries at every door. What is significant about this historic Council of Nicea, however, which Emperor Constantine himself urged the bishops to hold, is its condemnation of the Arian heresy (the idea that Christ is not fully God) and the proclamation of the Creed that is the prototype for all later Christian creeds — with its statement that Christ is "the only-begotten Son of God . . . *consubstantial* with the Father." The Christological foundations of the Faith, which have provided the basis for our belief in all the centuries since, were first codified there at Nicea.

Constantine was delighted with the whole thing. "You are the bishops inside the Church," he is said to have remarked to the council Fathers. "I am the bishop outside the Church." A theologically unsophisticated bishop, however, as proven by the letters he wrote to Arius and his great Catholic opponent Athanasius. "I find the cause [i.e., whether or not Christ is God] is trivial," he wrote. "Basically you think alike. . . . Remain united! . . . [T]he matter between you does not concern an essential point of faith." He could not have been more wrong, of course; so the council smiled politely and did its great work in spite of "the bishop outside."

Meanwhile, Constantine continued his checkered imperial career. Politically, he was the last of the truly great emperors, managing by stern measures to hold his crumbling realm together. His lurid personal life was less successful. He had Licinius executed because the Eastern emperor kept falling back into the habit of persecuting Christians, so there was now only one emperor of both East and West. He had his wife, Fausta, killed because he suspected her of adultery with his son Crispus (from a previous marriage), and he had that son killed too. He had prisoners of war tortured to death and a political enemy thrown to the lions.

His elderly mother, Helena, heartsick at the slaughter, made a famous pilgrimage of reparation to the Holy Land, where she was able, through both intelligent investigation and supernatural aid, to discover and have excavated the holiest sites of Christianity. Calvary, the True Cross, the Holy Sepulcher, and many more sites were Helena's discoveries. And thanks to her erection of churches above the sacred places, they remained identifiable even after the catastrophic loss of the Holy Land to the Arabs in the 700s.

The fateful division of the empire

Her son, meanwhile, was also turning his attention to the East. He wanted to move the capital of the empire to a small Greek trading outpost known as Byzantium, on the Bosporus straits near the Black Sea. It was an audacious idea, unthinkable to most Romans, and yet there were sound reasons in favor of it. Although it was nearer the frontiers from which the empire was then under sporadic attack, it could itself be made virtually impregnable. It was near all the major trade routes, whereas economically declining Italy was not. Constantine also had personal reasons for pushing this project: he distrusted the loyalty of Rome, in which he had many political enemies; perhaps, too, Rome reminded him of Crispus, Fausta, and his sins. Finally, although he might not yet have been baptized, he seems to have sincerely wanted to build a new city that would be Christian, not pagan, from its foundation — despite the pagan temples he also tolerated there.

The Edict of Milan and the Liberation of the Church

The city — New Rome, or Constantinople — was built in short order, and it did prove a wise decision, at least strategically. While the Western Empire fell to the barbarians in the following century, Constantinople and part of the Eastern Empire survived for another thousand years. On the other hand, the Latin civilization that Constantine thought he was transplanting failed to take deep root, and the East, which became known as Byzantium, became a Hellenized region: Greek-speaking, Greek-thinking, Greek in worship. The emperors of the East tended to dominate the Church in their realm to the point that it lost its independence from the state. Far from remaining the Catholic city of Constantine's dreams, Constantinople would go on to host one heresy after another. Increasingly touchy about its submission to the pope, the Eastern Church finally fell into the melancholy schism that still has not been mended.

There was one great benefit, perhaps unrecognized at the time, to the moving of the government apparatus to Constantinople: it left Rome to the Church. In view of what would happen to the Church in the East, the future Byzantine Empire, the papacy's possession of Rome was of inestimable value. In Constantinople, the Eastern emperors began to meddle more and more in Church affairs and to resent the authority of the popes in far-off Italy. Several of the early popes felt their dangerous wrath and were driven into exile or even killed because they refused to cede control of the Church to a temporal ruler. Of course, they would later face the same challenge from the kings of the West, particularly the German emperors, but they were far less vulnerable in Rome than they would have been had their headquarters been in a monarch's own city. The papacy would, in the future, acquire the Papal States as a territorial buffer zone to discourage invasion and would find champions among the turbulent array of tribes that supplanted

Roman rule in the West: Franks and Normans, in turn, would help defend the sovereign independence of the Vicar of Christ. It was thus providential that the See of Peter was separated from the seat of the emperors; this way, it could breathe freely and pursue its divine mission in relative peace and security.

As for the emperor who achieved all this, his spiritual life was full of ambiguity until the end. Earlier in his career, he seems to have tried to combine elements of Christian worship with a dash of paganism. Later on, he seemed to believe sincerely in Christianity and to pray a great deal, while also allowing pagan temples to be built in Constantinople and continuing the cult of the emperor, with its pagan priesthood. The question of his baptism is particularly vague. According to Eusebius and most modern historians, he remained a catechumen, and therefore unable to assist at the Holy Sacrifice of the Mass, until death was nearly upon him. Whatever the reason for this — and it was common at the time to defer baptism so as to go straight to heaven after death, without the chance of committing more sins — he left it until very late.

By 337, he had a definite presentiment that he was going to die of an illness he had contracted. Bishops assembled around his deathbed, and he explained that although he had hoped to be baptized in the Jordan, he would not delay any longer. His royal robes were exchanged for the white alb of one about to receive the sacrament. "Here is the day I have thirsted for so long," he murmured. "Here is the hour of salvation for which I have been waiting." Following his baptism, by an Arian bishop, he had time to say, "Now I am truly happy. I see the light divine." It was noon on Pentecost Sunday when he died.

Another view is drawn from a very ancient Roman tradition and inscription in the Lateran Basilica, and supported by the writings of Fathers and Doctors of the Church, scholars such as St.

Bede, and numerous others for over a thousand years. According to this version, Constantine was baptized in the Lateran by Pope St. Sylvester I, who came to the papal throne in 314. The emperor's Christian writings, speeches, and actions certainly date from his defeat of Maxentius, and if it were not for the account of Eusebius — touching and dramatically appealing — there might be no problem accepting the earlier date for his baptism. When we consider that the bishop who supposedly baptized him on his deathbed was an Arian, however, there remains the possibility that the story was an Arian lie, a propaganda piece intended to claim the great ruler for one of their own. (This is the kind of thing that causes historians to sneeze and brood over ancient, dusty tomes, searching for the one document that will cut the Gordian knot of hopelessly conflicting stories. Never mind. We will all know the truth someday.)

We need not follow the Roman Empire to its dissolution in the century following Constantine. The tale is one of economic, social, and cultural disintegration, and political and military impotence. One of the later emperors managed to reunite the empire, but only temporarily, while population decline caused the army to be so short of recruits that barbarians had to be taken into the ranks. And all the while, raids on the borders increased, Rome itself was sacked — to the shock and dismay of even Christian writers like Jerome and Augustine — and the end finally came in 476, with a Gothic chieftain replacing the last Roman emperor in the West. We will take a closer look at the invaders when we come to our next date.

The future of the liberated Church
So, was the period following the Edict of Milan a utopia for the Church? Far from it. Now, in fact, the Church faced challenges

even more formidable than persecution. The first was the depravity of late Roman society. We have seen the addiction of Romans to violent and obscene entertainment; private lives were often just as degraded. The native Roman reverence for marriage, motherhood, and family had nearly disappeared in the Late Empire, while homosexuality and pornographic "entertainment" had become prevalent, along with abortion and divorce.

Thus, when millions of citizens of the empire became Christians, along with the barbarians we will meet shortly, a peculiar problem arose for the Church. The masses of the converted (or the half-converted, who often joined the Church for mixed motives) were not instantly changed into fervent Catholics. Often they saw nothing wrong with their immoral way of life. Sometimes they tried to hedge their bets and keep a little reverence for the sun god in reserve, as Pope St. Leo was horrified to observe when he saw Catholics entering St. Peter's give a salute to the sun first. The danger was that this mass influx of the immoral and the lukewarm might drag down the whole Christian community. And we shall see that, in fact, this is what was to happen, in the Dark Ages.

The second peril, also more deadly than outright persecution, was heresy. The Council of Nicea dealt with the Arian heresy, but that was only one of numerous heresies in the early Church. Many were invented in the eastern provinces of the empire by subtle intellectuals, who tried to combine tenets of their favorite pagan philosophers with Christian doctrine, and ended by distorting and perverting it. On the other hand, Constantine's homeland of Britain would give rise to the fifth-century heresy of Pelagius, who denied both Original Sin and the necessity of grace for salvation. (When St. Lupus and St. Germanus finally succeeded in defeating this dangerous teaching in Britain, they attributed their victory to the proto-martyr St. Alban.)

The Edict of Milan and the Liberation of the Church

The now "above-ground Church," then, instead of entering an era of peace and tranquility following Constantine's edict, found itself confronted with masses of difficult converts whose hearts were hard to change; with clever doctrines seeking to supplant its own; with unwelcome pressure from the emperors in Constantinople; and finally, with the arrival of barbarian hordes that would bring still more headaches with them. This is, in fact, a preview of the rest of Catholic history. The breathing spaces are few and far between, and the Bride will achieve lasting peace and rest only at the eternal banquet of the Bridegroom. Satan will never cease trying to destroy what Christ has built, but he lacks originality: we will see that most of the Church's future problems will simply be variations on the themes just mentioned.

What is truly incredible — we would say it was impossible if we did not know otherwise — is that the Church would triumph in every crisis to come, and indeed we believe it must endure until the end of time. In every age, God raises up human allies of his cause: saints, of course, but also rough, sinful men who often seem unlikely choices for divine instruments. Constantine the Great is the first of them.

452 AD

St. Leo Repulses the Huns

Third-century Catholics might well have hoped, quite logically, that the conversion of Constantine and the liberation of the Church meant the beginning of a new Christian age for the Roman Empire. What was once the "whore of Babylon" in St. John's Apocalypse became Catholic Rome; surely it would be she who would spread the Gospel "to all nations"?

Yet this was not to be. Christianity would become the official religion of the Roman Empire before the fourth century ended and the new capital of Constantinople would no longer have even one pagan temple, but the empire was doomed. The western empire would end in misery and chaos in the century following Constantine; the East, left to itself, would survive another thousand years, but for most of that time, it would languish in schism and heresy. Why did all this happen?

An empire crumbling on every side
The causes for the collapse of the Western Empire have been endlessly discussed by historians, with some giving more weight to one thing and others to another. Certainly the economy was in crisis. Despite the draconian measures taken by Diocletian and continued by Constantine to increase revenues and meet the

rising costs of defending the borders, inflation was rampant, the soil was exhausted, and once-independent farmers found themselves sharecropping on the estates of local landowners — the serfs and lords of the future. The welfare budget grew out of control as city governments struggled to feed and entertain the urban proletariat, lest it explode in revolution. There were not enough qualified men going into the army — those in the urban underclasses were useless as soldiers — so barbarians began to make up a larger and larger percentage of both officers and fighting men. Many of these men had lived within the boundaries of the empire for generations and were thoroughly loyal to Rome; but some of them, especially from tribes recently allowed to settle within the borders, were of dubious loyalty. Faced with guarding a border against their own kin pushing from the other side, they might well open the gates — or at least look the other way.

Political life in the third and fourth centuries alternated between brief periods of stability and grim power struggles between various claimants for the imperial thrones of both East and West. The chronicles of these sordid rivalries often read more like the quarrels of savage tribes than of civilized men (although it is true that some of the political men of the time were barbarians). If you wanted to demoralize an opponent, you might send him the head of one of his friends in the mail — just one of the increasingly brutal practices that became common as Rome staggered on to its final collapse.

Above all, there were psychological and spiritual factors involved in the disintegration of the empire, some mentioned in the previous chapter. One historian has written of the "terrifying sluggishness of the whole population," and perhaps what is most appalling is that so many members of this population, including the politicians packing up the heads they had just cut off, were

Catholic. St. John Chrysostom's sermons describing the evil lives of the new Catholics of Constantinople show that things were no better over there. He inveighed against the indecent luxury of the rich, while the poor starved for want of alms. He described in detail extravagantly expensive households with their furniture of silver and ivory, and the sybaritic banquets at which guests were serenaded by flute girls of questionable morals. While praising the kindness of some Christian masters to their slaves, St. John also excoriated the everyday cruelty practiced by many others. It is depressing to read of these things, as well as of the survival of pagan customs among Christians and the sensuality and worldliness of the clergy.

More decadent than the barbarians

Indeed, conspicuous immorality was eating away at every part of imperial society. Following a Vandal raid in Africa probably in the 430s, Salvian of Marseilles contrasted the behavior of the barbarians with those of the Christian Romans. First he detailed the various vices that were rampant in Carthage: "More grave and criminal was the fact that those vices, about which the blessed Apostle Paul complained with the greatest lament of his soul, were almost all practiced in Africa. That is, men, having put aside the natural use of woman, burned in their desires for one another; men doing base things with men, and receiving to themselves the reward of their error which they should receive. . . . Did the blessed Apostle say this about barbarians and wild peoples? No indeed, but about us, that is, about the Romans in particular. . . ." Salvian was especially distressed that these things occurred in "a Christian city, in an ecclesiastical city, where the apostles taught with their own teaching. . . ." He laments that although the Romans' immorality dated from pre-Christian times, "it did not cease after the advent of the Gospels." Baptism alone did not make all, or even most, of previously decadent citizens of the empire into decent Christians.

As for the barbarians, Salvian asks, "Who, after all this, does not admire the Vandals?" They might have been expected to adopt the vices of the rich and corrupt lands they conquered, yet they had not done so — and "none of them became effeminate." After discussing how the Vandals rid Africa of both unnatural vice and, "for the time being," prostitution, Salvian asks, "What hope can there be for the Roman State when the barbarians are more chaste and more pure than the Romans? . . . What hope of pardon or of life can there be for us in the sight of God when we see chastity among the barbarians and are, ourselves, unchaste?" It was not the strength of the barbarians that caused the conquest, nor the physical and military weakness of the Romans. "The vices of our bad lives have alone conquered us."

None other than St. Augustine, addressing the people of Hippo during the brutal Vandal siege of that unfortunate African city, said, "Enough of your weeping and wailing! Are you not yourselves responsible for this fate which is overwhelming you? 'These are difficult and dreadful times,' people are saying. But these times are part of us, are they not? The times are what we have made them!"

It was therefore not just pagan Rome that was to be chastised in the fourth century. It was now Christian Rome. The instruments of divine punishment were to be the barbarians, pouring into the empire by hundreds of thousands, tribe after tribe overwhelming the border defenses. A preview of what this would mean had already occurred in the East at the Battle of Adrianople in 378. Visigoths who had been settled within the empire had been maltreated by Roman officials and took up arms in reprisal. Perhaps eager to have the glory of defeating them for himself, the eastern emperor Valens did not wait for the arrival of his colleague Gratian, emperor of the West, to begin the battle. A vivid blow-by-blow account of the debacle has come down to us from the Roman historian Ammianus Marcellinus, telling of the overwhelming force of the enemy cavalry, the hideous toll it took on the Roman forces, and the death of the emperor: "Scarcely one-third of the whole army escaped. Nor, except the battle of Cannae [216 BC], is so destructive a slaughter recorded in our annals."

In 410 another group of Visigoths sacked Rome itself. The inhabitants braced themselves for the usual indiscriminate slaughter and pillage that typically accompanied such events in the ancient world. The sack was indeed ghastly, but St. Augustine remarked on something new about this one. He called it a *nova more*, a new way of behaving. Some of the barbarian soldiers actually spared civilians, and even escorted them to churches set aside as places of sanctuary. The Visigoths did this because they were Christians — Arian heretics, but still Christian. This was a sign of tenuous hope for the future.

The Huns: a new kind of barbarian

It began to look as if those Romans who, we are told, were so despairing of their own society that they "prayed God to send them the barbarians" were going to get their wish. If it was apparent that the future of the West lay with the barbarians, there still remained an urgent question: Which barbarians? The Visigoths and other Germanic tribes had long been familiar to the Romans; many of them were Arian, but at least they were Christians of some kind. The Romans understood them to a large extent, and quite a few of them had come to appreciate the value of civilization. In the 400s, however, a more sinister threat loomed on the horizon. The mysterious people who had been responsible for the most massive of the German invasions around the empire appeared on the Roman scene in person. The Huns, in their six-thousand-mile trek across the steppes from Mongolia, had terrified the peoples they met to such an extent that they fell all over themselves scrambling for safety within the empire. For a while, the Huns held their peace, and some actually served in the Roman army. They could be seen in the streets of imperial cities, where Romans marveled at their strange appearance, clothes, and odor. This uneasy situation changed with the accession to the throne of the Huns in 435 of a ruthless genius named Attila.

The Roman historian Ammianus Marcellinus wrote about the Huns in the fourth century, before the accession of Attila, when they first appeared on the edges of the eastern empire after driving the Germanic tribes before them. "The seed-bed and origin of all this destruction and of the various calamities," wrote the historian, was "the Huns, who are mentioned only cursorily in ancient writers and who dwell beyond the Sea of Azov . . . near the frozen ocean, [and] are quite abnormally savage." Moreover, "They are totally ignorant of the distinction between right and wrong. . . . [T]hey are under no restraint from religion or superstition." Although Ammianus might have exaggerated to some extent, he certainly reflected the Roman perception of the Huns, as well as that of the tribes who fled them. He shows us Goths pleading desperately to be allowed into the Roman Empire to escape massacre by the Huns, and the foreboding of those already within the empire.

In the fifth century, the Byzantine historian Priscus described the Huns' frightening appearance, and how they had routed the tribe of the Alans "by the terror of their looks, inspiring them with no little horror by their awful aspect and by their horribly swarthy appearance. They have a sort of shapeless lump, if I may say so, not face, and pinholes rather than eyes." Short, bow-legged, and awkward when not on their tough and speedy steppe ponies, they practically lived on horseback. They conducted business from the backs of their steeds, ate half-raw meat that they warmed under their saddles while riding, and even slept in the saddle. Their strangeness, as well as their unfamiliar battle tactics — shooting their peculiar and deadly arrows with astonishing accuracy, scattering and reforming ranks with lightning speed on their unexpectedly swift horses — combined to terrify all who heard of them.

When Attila, a highly intelligent and talented man with a grand plan, began his rule, it was clear that the Hunnish menace to the Roman Empire had suddenly become far more serious. He set up headquarters in Pannonia, part of modern-day Hungary, and established a no-man's land of three days' march between his territory and the borders of the empire. He refused to allow Huns to serve in the Roman army and crucified those who disobeyed. Attila set about uniting all the tribes within the boundaries he had established and creating a joint German-Hun army. With this he intended to conquer the empire, whose defects and weaknesses he knew very well (he had once been a hostage in Rome, and he spoke Latin). Combined with the endless steppe lands the Huns had already subdued, Attila's dream empire would have been at least as large as the one that would be established by the Mongols in the thirteenth and fourteenth centuries.

We have a word picture of Attila that might be from the very chatty Priscus (who, as an imperial envoy, had considerable experience of the Huns), although it is found in the work of a later historian:

> He was a man born to shake the races of the world, a terror to all lands, who in some way or other frightened everyone

by the dread report noised abroad about him, for he was haughty in his carriage, casting his eyes about him on all sides so that the proud man's power was to be seen in the very movements of his body. A lover of war, he was personally restrained in action, most impressive in counsel, gracious to suppliants, and generous to those to whom he had once given his trust. He was short of stature with a broad chest, massive head, and small eyes. His beard was thin and sprinkled with grey, his nose flat, and his complexion swarthy, showing thus the signs of his origins.[2]

Attila had been dubbed by a monk "the Scourge of God," and seems to have been pleased with the sobriquet.

Once he was ready to move on the empire, he began on the eastern borders of the realm, destroying trading posts and cities on the Danube and extracting large ransoms from the Emperor Theodosius II. When this emperor's tougher successor, Marcian, refused to continue the ransom payments, Attila turned to the West.

His pretext for invasion was a rather incredible letter written to him by an imperial princess, Honoria, sending him a ring and a sum of money. It seems this strong-willed sister of the Emperor Valentinian had had an affair with a man with whom she might have planned to overthrow her brother. The plot was discovered, and a safe and sober match was arranged for her, which she absolutely rejected. Hence the idea of writing to the fierce barbarian for help in avoiding the hated marriage (her mother had done something similar many years earlier, so it ran in the family.) Attila might have construed the ring, not as a guarantee of the sender's identity, but as a proposal of marriage, and been intrigued by his (erroneous) idea that Honoria's dowry was half the Western

Empire. He did not respond immediately, but when he was ready to attack the West, this would be his excuse.

In any case, early in 451 the Huns moved on Gaul with a large number of the German allies Attila had recruited. The panic they spread was such that events are hard to sort out, but it is clear that the slaughter was great and the number of cities sacked or destroyed considerable. Some were spared: at Troyes, Attila was persuaded by the holy bishop St. Lupus not to harm the city; the bishop himself was taken hostage by the Huns but survived. (Ironically, he was then banished from his see for a couple of years on the grounds of collaboration with the enemy.)

At Paris it was an extraordinary woman who rallied the terror-stricken inhabitants. St. Genevieve — future patron saint of the city — was then about thirty, living a life of charity and prayer as a virgin consecrated to God. When the Huns approached, she promised the inhabitants that if they did penance, the city would be spared. Addressing the women, she declared, "Let the men flee if they want to, if they are incapable of fighting. We women will pray so hard that God will surely hear our prayers!" And God heard, and the Huns did not attack Paris.

The pope, bishops, Romans,
and barbarians unite in a common cause

In 451 the Huns were approaching the city of Orléans, south of Paris, when they met with their first serious resistance. The half-Roman general Aetius had scraped together an army made up of what was left of the Roman legions as well as representatives of numerous barbarian tribes — one of which he had just defeated. Romans and barbarians alike saw the Huns as the greatest threat they faced and were willing to join forces against them. The Church was not absent from this common effort against the Huns, although its decisive effort would not be seen until the following year. Meanwhile, the Bishop of Orléans alerted Aetius to the approach of the Huns, while another bishop negotiated an agreement with the Visigoths, bringing them into the coalition.

The chroniclers of the all-day battle that ensued place the number of casualties on both sides between 160,000 and 300,000 men. Even accounting for the unreliability of ancient statistics, this indicates a titanic struggle that was costly to all the participating peoples. The Huns retired to their camp, considerably weakened, and then withdrew across the Rhine. They were not finished, however, not by any means.

In the spring of 452 Attila invaded Italy. Town after town fell, the population fleeing for their lives. Aquileia, on the Adriatic, was so large and well-fortified that it took the Huns three months of siege to conquer it. They took a grim revenge for the inconvenience: a hundred years later, its ruins could scarcely be located. Some of the inhabitants of the city and its surroundings were able to flee into the marshes and islands, and their settlements later became Venice. Meanwhile, Manua, Padua, Milan, and many other towns and cities fell to the invaders, brought down by siege or opening their gates in despair.

The imperial court had for some time made its headquarters at Ravenna, considering it more secure than Rome. With the approach of the Huns, however, Emperor Valentinian did not wait to test Ravenna's defenses; the court fled south to Rome. The Scourge of God now seemed about to fall on both the Church and the state; Rome would go the way of Aquileia. It seems that the emperor then asked Pope Leo's help in this crisis, and the pontiff agreed. He must have been storming heaven with his prayers for the deliverance of the city, like another Abraham interceding for Sodom. He certainly had no illusions about the virtues of the populace and would not have considered Rome's destruction un-merited. Nor did he have any illusions about the intentions of At-tila, who seemed bent on the devastation and occupation of Italy. But, "The only hope of salvation," wrote St. Prosper of Aquitaine, Leo's friend and secretary, "was to count on the mercy of a king without mercy." Leo prayed, and he set forth to meet the enemy. His plan was to meet the Huns in the north, to try to head off their advance on Rome and prevent the further devastation of Italy.

Attila and his army were at the river Mincio, in northern Italy, when they saw an odd procession approaching from the other side. Priests, monks, and other clergy were marching toward the Huns, chanting and carrying monstrances and crosses. There were also a consul, an ex-prefect, and other governmental officials empow-ered to negotiate with the enemy. Attila rode into the river as far as a small island, from which he called to the leader of the proces-sion, asking his name. "I am Leo, the pope." The Hun proceeded to the other side of the river, and the two men spoke. "Attila," St. Prosper tells us, "received the legation with dignity, and he was so delighted with the presence of this pope that he decided to abandon the war and retire across the Danube, after having prom-ised peace." No one knows exactly what was said, but when Leo returned to Rome, he merely told the emperor, "Let us give thanks to God, for he has saved us from a great danger."

While the pope's arguments are unknown, historians have as-sumed that the Roman officials who accompanied him offered the Huns some form of ransom. This had always been the means of buying off barbarian attacks, and it would have provided the Huns with enough provisions to leave Italy quickly. They then with-drew from Italy, threatening to return if Honoria were not deliv-ered to their king. Attila seems then to have made a halfhearted attack on Gaul and been repulsed by the Visigoths. He then retired to Pannonia, from where, according to Priscus, he began to badger the eastern emperor with threats of invasion and demands for tribute. An embassy sent from Constantinople was badly received at the court of the Huns, and things began to look grim for the eastern empire as the Huns prepared for their next move.

Fortunately for both East and West, in 453 Attila took yet another wife and shortly thereafter met his unusual fate. As Priscus recounts: "Worn out by excessive merriment at his wedding and sodden with sleep and wine, he lay on his back. In this position a hemorrhage, which ordinarily would have flowed from his nose, since it was hindered from its accustomed channels poured down his throat in deadly passage and killed him. So drunkenness put a shameful end to a king famed in war." In the power struggle that resulted among the many sons of Attila, the German tribes that had been part of his army broke free and the whole Hunnish enterprise fell apart. God would use this Scourge to chastise his people no longer.

As for Pope St. Leo, Doctor of the Church, victor over several of the most dangerous heresies the Church had faced, he went back to work in Rome. In thanksgiving for deliverance from the Huns, he overthrew a statue of Jupiter and had it turned into the famous statue of St. Peter, still venerated today in St. Peter's Basilica. Unlike Sodom, Rome had been spared by God. There might not have been many "just men" in it, but there certainly was at least one. Three years later, Leo was again called upon to negotiate with a would-be conqueror, Genseric the Vandal, who was besieging the city. He proved less amenable than Attila to the pope's persuasion, but even so, given Genseric's record for "vandalism," the results were amazing. He confined himself to looting the city and agreed not to burn it, murder the inhabitants, or destroy the ancient monuments. (For a Vandal, that represented remarkable self-control.)

The meaning of it all

Historians have argued that the Huns were moved to leave Italy for reasons other than the confrontation with Leo. The climate was unhealthy; they might have been short on food; some of their advisors pointed out to Attila that Alaric had died within a few weeks of sacking Rome, and Attila was superstitious. (Leo, in fact, might have offered all these arguments, to his credit.) Against this is the record of the Huns' progress in Italy up to their arrival at Rome, and the fact that they seemed to have been looking forward to the spectacular loot they would acquire from the great city. Attila, after all, had been there; he knew what it was worth.

Even if other reasons passed through the Hun king's brain, however, it was the pope's embassy that made him pause and allow himself to be persuaded to withdraw. It seems plain that the Scourge of God was finally deflected because God heard the prayers of St. Leo and inspired his words. Two results followed from this. First, those diehard pagans who had been complaining that the barbarians had come because of the substitution of Christianity for the worship of the gods of Rome were answered. Christ, not Jupiter, had saved Rome, in the person of his vicar — a point St. Leo hammered home with the hammering of Jupiter's statue into another shape.

Second, the destiny of Europe was not to be a province of Asia, the tributary of a great Empire of the steppes; that fate would befall Russia and many other states under Mongol rule, but the West had a different future. At the moment, no doubt, it looked bleak, but the struggle with the Huns had brought out unexpected signs of hope. Romans and barbarians were able to cooperate with each other in resisting a common aggressor, and the future of Christendom lay in that cooperation. The role of the Church, particularly of the saints such as St. Lupus, St. Genevieve, and St. Leo, was also a preview of the new Catholic Europe that would slowly and painfully emerge from the wreckage of the empire, under the leadership of the papacy.

496 AD

The Baptism of Clovis Gives Birth to France

For another quarter-century after the withdrawal of the Huns, the Roman Empire in the West lurched through more crises and Germanic invasions. Finally the last emperor was deposed in 476 and a German chief, Odoacer (or Odovacer), became king of Italy — the first king Rome had seen since it overthrew the hated Etruscan kings in 509 BC. This date is often taken to mark the end of the Roman Empire in the West. Although the term "fall of Rome" can be debated, nuanced, modified, and turned into something else, it is clear that a milestone was reached in 476. Everywhere in the former provinces of the empire, the chiefs and kinglets of the many tribes carved out territories for themselves where Roman organization and Roman law had once held sway.

All institutions suffered during this time of confusion, and the Church was no exception. But the main problem posed to the Church by the change in rulers of the empire was not the barbarians themselves but their religion: nearly all were Arians.

Barbarian Arianism

This crude cult had been spread among the northern tribes by Arian missionaries fleeing the empire after the condemnation of the Arian heresy (which held that Jesus was not truly divine) at the Council of Nicea in 325. Its persistence was due to the extraordinary efforts of the third-century Goth Ulfilas, who seems to have had Greek ancestry and was raised a Catholic. Educated and intelligent, he visited Constantinople as a young man and there took up Arianism. He received episcopal consecration from an Arian Byzantine bishop and returned to spend seven years spreading the heresy among his people. Ulfilas was a determined and ingenious missionary. He invented a Gothic script, and translated the Scriptures into Gothic, which was also used in Arian rituals. Thus, Christianity (if a sect that denies the divinity of Christ can be called that) became a simple religion among the German warriors. It was short on theology, but its rituals appealed to the barbarian taste for midnight rites in the woods with lots of singing. Its ethics emphasized courage and other warrior traits. Not only did this transformed Arianism bring no civilization with it (the refined Arius would have had trouble recognizing it), but it was imbued with hostility toward Roman culture and the Catholic Church.

The Catholic missionary counterattack also made use of the Gothic language and script, and managed to reclaim some souls for the Church. On the whole, however, the fifth-century rulers of Spain, Italy, and many other former Roman provinces were Arian in worship and mentality. The attitude of Arian conquerors toward the Catholic peoples they vanquished varied. Some actively persecuted Catholics, some barely tolerated them, others were more flexible. Everywhere, however, they seem to have looked down on Catholicism as the inferior religion of a conquered people. Not an encouraging situation for Catholicism in the West.

The Franks move in

There was a major exception to the popularity of Arianism among the barbarians, one group that stood out from the Arian sea and remained staunchly pagan: this was the tribe of the Franks, who had settled on the banks of the Rhine and in northern Gaul. In the fifth century, they were no more sympathetic to Rome and the Church than their Arian neighbors. It is true that sometimes they had fought on the Roman side when it suited them. But they carried a vague grudge out of the dim past — a tradition of mistreatment by a Roman governor — against Roman rule. And they usually had too much to do with defending their territory from other tribes and fighting among themselves to be of any use to Rome.

Yet these unlikely pagans would become, not only the champions of Catholicism, but the future saviors of classical civilization. If ever there was a divine surprise in history, this was it — and it began only a few years after the official "fall" of Rome, in the last decades of the fifth century.

Who were the Franks? Apparently the name refers to a collection of tribes from the area of the Baltic seacoast. One group of this conglomeration, the Salian Franks, invaded Gaul (modern France), of which part was still under shaky Roman control. They seem to have ruled part of northern Gaul with Roman approval, and moved south and west as Roman troops were gradually withdrawn between 455 and 475. The people the Franks found living in southern Gaul were Gallo-Romans — Catholics with strong ties to Rome and to Roman culture, although Christian missionaries found that converting those in the countryside went slowly. Even in the fifth century, there were plenty of pagans left in Gaul. The Church was, however, a strong presence in the region, particularly in the towns and cities. Often it was only the bishops who had the administrative ability to keep public services operating, and the populace looked to them for both spiritual and material assistance. The Church's esteemed and influential presence would play a crucial role when a young Frankish king took the throne.

The bishop and the king

By the 470s, the Merovingian (so named after a semi-legendary ancestor, Merovech) family had acquired a dominant position in Gaul, although quarrels and sporadic warfare continued between them and related families, as well as non-Frankish tribes.

Clovis was a precocious fifteen-year-old when he became king of the Salian Franks in 482. In Frankish, the name of this energetic warrior was Chlodovech — source of the name Ludovicus, or Louis, thus making Clovis the first of the many great French kings of that name. An incident from 486 gives a glimpse into the young king's personality. His soldiers had pillaged many churches and had borne away from one a vase that St. Gregory of Tours described as being "of marvelous size and beauty." The bishop sent a request to Clovis, asking that, if nothing else, might the vase be restored to him? Clovis agreed, but before he could return it, one of his soldiers — piqued at not getting the vase for himself — raised his battleaxe and smashed it. Clovis said nothing but patiently delivered the damaged object to the bishop. A year later, however, while reviewing his troops, he criticized the vase-smasher for the condition of his weapons and threw one of them on the ground. The man bent to pick it up, and Clovis smashed his skull saying, "Thus did you do to the vase." A pretty ruthless kid. But even then, it seems, somewhat favorably disposed toward the Church.

At his accession, St. Remigius, the great and energetic Bishop of Reims, saw fit to write the young king a most interesting letter:

> Great news has reached us. You have just been placed at the
> head of the Frankish armies. None are surprised to see you

become what your fathers were. What matters first of all is to respond to the designs of that Providence that rewards your merit by raising you to the heights of honor, and this is the occasion for justifying the proverb, "A work is crowned by its end." Take for counselors those whose choice does honor to your discernment. Be prudent, chaste, moderate; honor bishops and do not disdain their advice. As long as you live on good terms with them, the affairs of state will prosper. Raise up the soul of your peoples, relieve the widows, feed the orphans. Later on they will serve you, and thus you will conquer the hearts of the very ones who fear you. Let justice be done both in your heart and by your lips. . . . Let your praetorium be open to all, and let the humblest petition be heard there. You now possess the power that was your father's; use it to deliver captives and console the oppressed. Remember that in your audiences no one should see himself as a foreigner. To your pleasures and games invite, if you like, young men of your own age, but only discuss business matters with the elders. It is thus that you will reign gloriously.[3]

This letter is fascinating from several points of view. Not once does it mention the Catholic Faith, nor urge the young pagan to convert. (A recent historian has called it an example of the "Roman attitude" that Christianity was not for barbarians, and calls the tone of the letter "aloof." This is certainly a novel view, and there are many adjectives I would wish to apply to it, were I not restraining myself.) Putting aside the idiotic suggestion that the Church was not interested in converting the barbarians (which would require an explanation of what St. Patrick and all the other Dark Age missionaries thought they were doing), the letter appears as a model of ecclesial discretion and pastoral psychology. St. Remigius must have heard something of the impetuous character and personality of the teenage king; perhaps there had already been other incidents like the affair of the vase. He would also have known that Clovis might be susceptible to influence by his Arian sister. Not knowing exactly how far that influence had gone, he would have wished to tread cautiously in establishing friendly relations. Above all, he would have been careful to avoid antagonizing a willful youngster. He must also have known that the barbarians were often in awe of spiritual authority, and that the sights and sounds of Catholic ceremony, as well as the clergy themselves, greatly impressed them. Rather than make a heavy-handed demand for conversion by this very young and very busy ruler, then, the bishop chose to plant in his mind a few simple — but significant — ideas.

First, the illustrious head of the Church at Reims expresses his pleasure at the news of the boy's accession (subtext: the Church is inclined to support him). Second, it is Providence that has raised up this king and Providence that has a plan for him. (Clovis would probably wonder what this "Providence" and its plan are. Possibly those bishops he is supposed to consult could tell him?) Third, things will go well for him if he maintains good relations with them. (And suppose he does not? Is there a very delicate threat implied? Will the unknown God of these impressive prelates take revenge on him?) Finally, the king should follow not only principles of natural law, but also what can only be called Christian morality: a call to a way of behaving that would be distinctly novel for a Frank, but just might appeal to whatever idealism lurked within his warrior soul.

Paris and Genevieve
One can easily imagine that Clovis was impressed with this letter; at the very least, he was not a boy who got a lot of mail, and

any letter would have gotten his attention. Clovis proceeded to defeat both a rival Frankish tribe to the east of Gaul and the last shreds of Roman authority in western Gaul. He then proceeded to take over, piece by piece, almost the whole of Gaul — the equivalent of most of modern France. Soon the Franks made up perhaps a quarter of the population of the territory, and fortunately they were not out to exterminate the Gallo-Romans or destroy everything they saw, as the Vandals had been. In the course of conquering Gaul, he naturally thought he would take Paris, too — the ancient *Lutetia* of the Romans where the Emperor Julian loved to stay.

Unfortunately for him, St. Genevieve was still going strong and still popular with the Parisians for her holiness, her miracles, and for having rallied them against the Huns over forty years earlier. She was near seventy now, but as energetic as ever, and she would not open the gates to a pagan any more than she would to a Hun. She had sworn that barbarians would never set foot in her city. Thus, when Clovis laid siege to the city, his only hope was to starve it out.

The Parisians stayed behind the strong walls of their island, entirely surrounded by water, and Clovis had neither boats nor the means to build them quickly. The situation for the besieged became critical, and people began to starve. Then Genevieve herself managed to take twelve supply ships up the Seine to a town where she could fill them with supplies (almost absent-mindedly working many miracles of healing as she went), then returned to save her city.

Clovis gave up. St. Genevieve had kept the barbarians at the gates. But she prayed earnestly for the conversion of Clovis. Meanwhile another strong woman, Clotilda — perhaps in answer to the prayers of the saint of Paris — had entered the king's life.

Ten Dates Every Catholic Should Know

Clotilda changes her husband

This most attractive saint, the Catholic daughter of a Burgundian king, had grown up amidst the grim violence of the time while managing to preserve both piety and virtue. She was one of that considerable number of Christian women who willingly married barbarians in the hope of converting them. When Clovis sought Clotilda's hand, she did not object — whatever her private reservations might have been. They were married in 491 or 492, when he was in his early twenties and she was about seventeen. Possibly to her surprise, Clovis obviously esteemed her highly, and they became a devoted and loving couple. He remained steadfastly pagan, however, worshiping the gods of the Franks. The years went by, and Clovis still remained a pagan, even as he became increasingly impressed with the faith of his young wife (despite watching their first child die of illness shortly after he consented to have him baptized). He also greatly esteemed her spiritual advisor: Remigius, Bishop of Reims, who had sent the king that letter on his accession.

Clovis is said to have visited the shrine of St. Martin of Tours on November 11 of one year in the late 490s, on the saint's feast day, and witnessed miracles there that naturally impressed him. He gave no sign of abandoning paganism, though, until he became engaged in a particularly difficult battle with an enemy tribe, possibly the Alemanni, and an inspiration came to him: he would pray to "Clotilda's God" for victory. "Jesus Christ," the chronicler reports him as crying out, "Thou Who art, according to Clotilda, the Son of the living God, help me in my distress! If Thou dost give me victory, I will believe in Thee and I will be baptized." Like Constantine at the Battle of the Milvian Bridge, Clovis was victorious. He began to consider seriously who this God could be, obviously more powerful than the gods of the Franks or the Alemanni; and he sought religious instruction from St. Remigius.

The Baptism of Clovis Gives Birth to France

An epochal conversion

Both king and bishop seem to have been somewhat anxious as to what the effect of the ruler's conversion would be on his followers. It was not the Frankish people as a whole that caused concern; they seem to have been indifferent both to the Faith and to the gods their chiefs worshiped. The close associates of the king — the warriors of his inner circle — were another matter. So intimately were they associated with him in all their undertakings that the sudden change of religion on the part of their leader might well alienate them. "I would willingly hear you," Clovis is said to have told the bishop, but he hesitated; he seems to have been really convinced that his men would not want to abandon their gods. He dealt with the issue by summoning the men, explaining his plans to them, and asking their opinion. Unanimously, they agreed to abandon their old gods and accept the One preached by St. Remigius; since Clovis knew them well and yet did not expect this, it seems another example of extraordinary grace at work.

Baptism at the time was usually administered at Easter, but an exception was made in this case and the date set for Christmas; the traditional year of 496 might be incorrect, but at the most, it would have been within a few years of that date. It does not matter. What does matter is that it marked the beginning of Catholic France. In all of the West, Clovis would be the only Catholic king, already referred to by some as "the second Constantine."

On the threshold of the baptistery, the splendor of the vestments, the brilliantly lit church, and the litanies and hymns caused the overawed king to ask the saint, "Is this it, the kingdom of heaven you promised me?"

"No," Remigius replied, "but it is the beginning of the road that leads there."

Into the cathedral moved the solemn procession, the bishop and the king together, followed by Clotilda, her heart no doubt overflowing with joy and gratitude. More family members who were to be baptized followed, including both the sisters of Clovis; the Arian one did not need to be baptized, but received confirmation. Then came the three thousand Franks who had agreed to be baptized with their chief.

The famous words of the great bishop to the king just prior to his reception of the sacrament have come down to us: "It is well, great Sicambrian; bow down the neck with meekness, adore what thou hast thitherto burned and burn what thou hast adored."

During the baptismal ceremony, a striking incident occurred that was to have consequences for fifteen hundred years. In the fifth century, it was the custom to administer the sacrament of confirmation at the same time as baptism, and the moment had come during the ceremony when the bishop needed the holy chrism with which to anoint the king. The cathedral was so packed that it was hard to move, and the cleric carrying the holy oil could not get through the crowd. St. Remigius looked up to heaven to see a dove descending, a phial of oil in its beak. With this oil he anointed the king, and it was afterward used in the coronation ceremonies of the kings of France. (Gibbon, recounting the incident with his usual sneer, remarked that it was still used in his day — around 1780.) Smashed during the French Revolution, the remains were recovered and a few precious drops last used for the coronation of Charles X in 1824.

What are we to make of this? Many historians, even Catholic ones, have dismissed it as legend. They point out that it first appears in the writings of the great Archbishop Hincmar in the early 800s, and that it lacks plausibility; it is simply too marvelous to believe. On the other hand, libraries full of Dark Age documents have been lost to us, although records of the fifth century might not have been lost to the ninth. In the case of Hincmar, we must remember that he was Archbishop of *Reims*, where the miracle is said to have occurred. He could well have had access to contemporary records, perhaps written by St. Remigius himself. The account that has come down to us recounts one miraculous occurrence; it is not embellished with fantastic details, as are many false miracle stories, and it appeals to eyewitness testimony. The saints and kings of France believed it. I see no reason why such a supernatural sign, source of the custom of a sacred anointing of the French kings, might not have truly occurred. It would have solidified the faith of the newly baptized, added to the prestige of both bishop and king, and served as a symbol of God's favor for the monarchy of the "Eldest Daughter of the Church."

Once the barbarian king was properly baptized and anointed, St. Genevieve opened the gates and welcomed the royal couple to their new capital. For the rest of her life, she was their supporter and counselor, and a special friend of Clotilda — a young saint and an old saint, both great figures in the history of France. Clovis continued, like Constantine, his dual career as warrior king and Catholic champion. He even, as Constantine had at Nicea, called for a council: the Council of Orléans, where the bishops of Gaul would meet and discuss common problems. The Frankish people did not wake up Catholics the morning after their king's baptism, but their conversion rapidly followed. Such was the prestige of the king and his warriors that the missionary efforts of the Church soon bore abundant fruit throughout Gaul.

Why the baptism of Clovis mattered

The conversion of the Franks proved to be of enormous importance for the future of Catholic Europe. Catholicism was no longer the weak and inferior religion of the conquered. It was plain to pagans and Arians alike that the God of the Catholics was far stronger than theirs, since he gave his followers such spectacular victories. On this barbaric habit of thought the Church was able to build. Bishops, priests, monks, and wandering saints had all reinforced the positive attitude of occupied Gaul to the Frankish occupiers, and actively assisted and befriended the conquerors. This alliance between Catholic champions and the personnel of the Church would mean the eventual conversion of the whole continent — although it would take long, weary centuries of fighting and labor to achieve it.

St. Gregory of Tours, to whom we are indebted for the history of this period, although he wrote in the following century, was distressed at how full of violence and cruelty the Frankish world, and the Frankish court, remained even after its conversion. Neither the Franks nor their kings became exemplary Catholics overnight; neither had the Romans before them. Many of the deeds of Clovis himself seem brutal and of questionable morality, but the Church was patient. As St. Remigius said, "Much should be pardoned to one who has made himself the propagator of the Faith and the savior of the provinces." Again one is reminded of Constantine. Newly baptized Franks were also far too apt to carry pagan charms and invoke old pagan spirits, but again the Church was patient with them, as it had been with the Romans in similar circumstances.

Backsliding, and a glimmer of hope

St. Clotilda retired to a convent after the death of her husband, deeply grieved at the fratricidal warfare of her sons and the deaths of her grandsons. The post-Clovis period looked more than bleak, as the Frankish kingdom seemed to be disintegrating into warring factions, but just before her own death, Clotilda is said to have had the joy of meeting, or at least hearing about, her successor as saintly queen of the Franks. King Clotaire, a violent man who had succeeded to the throne of his father, Clovis, had taken captive a young girl of the Thuringian royal family in the course of a war he waged there in her eastern German land. Brought back to France, raised and educated there, young Radegund discovered the Catholic Faith, and it transformed her whole being. It was with reluctance that she wed the king at his insistence, but her reign rivals that of St. Elizabeth and other saintly queens for its charity and holiness. She would leave her royal spouse, with his permission, when he killed her own brother, and became as exemplary a nun as she had been a queen. She was not the last of the holy queens of France whose prayers and example, joined with those of other holy women like St. Genevieve, helped — far more than the bloody warfare of barbarian chiefs — to build the future Christendom of the West. That, however, was still far in the future.

800 AD

The Coronation of Charlemagne, Father of Christendom

The next great figure to stride onto the stage of history is outsized in every way. He towers over his contemporaries — literally — because he is over six feet tall, and his curly, reddish-brown hair and mustache make him even more imposing. If we agree to ignore his little squeaky voice, he is great in almost every other sense of the word as well: a great warrior, a great king and emperor, a great champion of the Church, a great patron of learning, a great promoter of economic revival. He is the Great Charles — protector of Rome, unifier of Europe, and Father of Western Christendom. It is hard to think how Catholic Europe would have emerged from the Dark Ages without him.

That Charles was a cradle Catholic was due to Clovis and the conversion of his people, for the future Charlemagne was a Frank. He was not, however, of the family of Clovis. In the more than two centuries that had elapsed between the death of Clovis and the accession of Charles, the Frankish royal family had gone rapidly downhill. Not only had the Merovingians, as they were called, made a habit of fratricidal warfare and palace intrigues; they had also become thoroughly dissolute and incompetent. One needs a strong stomach to read the record of their adventures and atrocities, recorded by St. Gregory of Tours and other contemporaries.

The deeds of some of their women — Brunhilda, Fredegund, and others — equal or surpass those of the men for gruesomeness. There is an account in St. Gregory of Tours' history of a Merovingian woman who wanted to get rid of her daughter-in-law. She opened a large and heavy chest, full of bolts of pretty cloth, and bade the younger woman examine them. When the unsuspecting girl knelt by the chest and bent forward, her mother-in-law neatly bundled her into the chest, slammed the lid, and sat upon it until she was sure that only an ex-daughter-in-law and some pieces of cloth were still within.

About Brunhilda, wife of a grandson of Clovis, there is too much nastiness to tell here. For several decades, she was a ruthless political power among the Franks, working for the interests of her husband, children, and grandchildren, until at length, when she was close to eighty, her crimes caught up with her. Put on trial, she was held responsible for numerous deaths, including those of several kings, clerics, and at least one canonized bishop (St. Didier). She was either broken on the rack or torn apart by four horses — accounts vary — and "finally," reports St. Gregory, "she died." We are far from the days of Clotilda here.

Decadence and nasty behavior were not the only problems of the Frankish rulers. After Clovis's death in 511, his kingdom of Francia had splintered into a sporadically united number of pieces. After 639, when Dagobert — the last really capable king — died, the Merovingians came to be called "the do-nothing kings," and this was an apt description. But if the kings were not doing their job, who was? It seems that some Merovingian had the sense to realize his own incompetence and entrust the running of his state to an official called the mayor of the palace; thereafter the kings were left to their depraved pastimes, occasionally trotted out for a carriage ride in public, while the mayors governed the kingdom. They did not ask for more.

The mayors of the palace

The family that came to provide the Frankish kings with their mayors can be traced back to two brothers, one of whom became a saint: St. Arnulf, of the clan known as the Arnulfings. Arnulf came from a distinguished Frankish family, and after receiving his education, he was sent to court to prepare for a position in the government. He was so competent that he served in both military and civil capacities, and in due course he married and had two sons. He had longed to devote his life to God as a religious, but when the episcopal see of Metz became vacant, he was made bishop, although he continued to play a role in political affairs (we are not told what became of his wife; she was presumably dead by this time.) He was kept busy trying to maintain peace among the Frankish kings, tutoring and advising the young king Dagobert, and working for the public good. At last it all began to get to him, and when he found someone to succeed him as bishop, he gladly retired to the mountains, to live out his remaining years in simplicity and religious contemplation.

This skilled and holy man would go on to do Europe one last service. Through his grandson Pepin II, or Pepin of Heristal, Arnulf became the founder of one of the great dynasties of Christendom: the Carolingians.

Pepin II

As mayor of the palace of the king of Austrasia — the eastern part of the former realm of Clovis — Pepin II proved an effective military leader in increasing the power of his king against Neustria, that western part of Francia that had been the former center of Merovingian power. During his term as mayor from 680 to 714, he also took charge of defense efforts against marauding tribes from the north and east. One of the greatest benefits he provided to his people was encouraging missionary activity among them; it was he who invited the great St. Wilibrod to come from England and begin his extraordinary career among the pagans in the areas newly conquered by the mayor: modern Belgium, Luxembourg, Holland, and parts of Germany. Wilibrod founded schools and monasteries, with the support of both the Frankish government and the pope, and was finally made bishop of the area in which he had labored.

Charles "the Hammer"

When Pepin died, his successor was his illegitimate son Charles, Carolus in Latin (from which the name Carolingian comes). His immediate goal was to continue his father's policy of defending the territory of Austrasia from the many restless tribes on its borders. Like Pepin, he also depended on missionaries to convert, and tame, the turbulent peoples in the neighborhood. Wilibrod was his friend, as he had been his father's, and he was soon reinforced by the arrival of another zealous English missionary, St. Boniface, destined to die a martyr's death. The chosen field of this great saint was the German areas east of the Rhine, where attachment to the old pagan gods and resistance to conversion were particularly strong.

Boniface was an early apologist as well as evangelist; his arguments against the German pagan gods showed him to be astute and intelligent, as well as charitable. In the organization of missionary activities, Boniface favored an innovative approach that was to have many positive consequences. He established monasteries in the wilderness, where the monks would clear the dense forests and farm, preach, and teach. Peasants were attracted to the cleared land and learned farming techniques from the religious; villages and parishes were formed; the forests were no longer sacred to the tribal gods, and conversions slowly increased. The monks were teachers, doctors, and advisors to all, and they did an enormous amount of good.

All of this Charles supported and encouraged, while he tirelessly organized and administered the kingdom of the Franks. (For a while he even did without a king, and apparently nobody missed him.) Perhaps his greatest challenge, however, came with the Muslim assault on Francia.

A few decades earlier, a tidal wave of Arabs and their North African allies had burst upon Christendom, East and West. In the West, it faced the decadent and ignorant peoples of the barbarian kingdoms; in Spain these fell quickly under Muslim control despite heroic resistance in some places. Only in the Asturias Mountains to the northwest did a little band of Catholic Visigoths manage to survive undefeated: the seed of the long, slow Spanish *Reconquista*, which was to come much later. The Mediterranean was a Muslim lake; Italy was repeatedly raided, and the southern coasts of Europe were unsafe.

When most of Spain had fallen to them, the Muslims began to raid across the Pyrenees into Aquitaine — a southeastern area of Francia that acknowledged Merovingian rule in an off-again, on-again way. In the early seventh century, its duke, Eudo, was allied with Charles, and now he was hard pressed by the Muslim attacks and required help urgently. Charles mustered an army drawn from all over the Frankish kingdom, and he did it in the nick of time; had the Franks remained in their earlier disarray, the peril that was approaching them from the south might have swept them away — as it had already swept away so much of what was formerly Christian.

The Battle of Tours saves Christian Europe

Bordeaux had been burned, and the Muslim forces were moving north. Their commanders had considered what sort of resistance they might meet with, and they are said to have had a low opinion of the Franks. This seemed to be corroborated when they routed Duke Eudes of Aquitaine — who fled — and were able to destroy churches and pillage his lands with impunity. Soon they had nearly reached Tours and its great shrine of St. Martin, perilously near the borders of Neustria, with its main city of Paris. It was there, somewhere between Tours and Poitiers, that Charles and the Frankish army engaged them. It was the year 732, one hundred years since the death of Mohammed had touched off the whirlwind that was still devastating the civilized world.

Instead of attacking, as was the Frankish custom, Charles had his men take a stand. They were warmly dressed — it was a crisp day in late October — and the Muslims must have been shivering in the light garb they had worn since they left Spain. A Spanish writer, called the "Pseudo-Isidore," aptly describes their assault on the Frankish line as breaking against "a wall of ice." The line held until nightfall, when the battle ceased. The Christian forces, glimpsing the tents of the Moors in the dawning light of the following day, presumed the fight would continue. But struck by the silence in the enemy camp, they sent out spies and learned that it had been abandoned. This seemed too good to be true, so they scouted out the whole surrounding countryside and found that the Moors had indeed vanished: the battle was won. As for Duke Eudes, he redeemed himself by joining Charles's forces and fighting bravely.

Was this one of those crucial battles that saved Western civilization? It is true that the work of finally expelling Muslim bands from the far south of Francia would go on for some time; Charles himself was later forced to confront a band of them in Burgundy, pursuing them down to the Mediterranean. Some historians have attempted to diminish the battle's importance by arguing that the Moorish expedition northward was only a raid, not an attempt to conquer Western Europe.

Yet that point seems irrelevant. Had the raid succeeded, there is every reason to think that the weakness of the Franks would have been followed up with conquest. Why should the conquerors of Persia, Syria, Egypt, Spain, North Africa, and much else stop if the way to Paris lay open? In any event, they were decisively defeated at Tours and did not renew the attempt. Christendom rejoiced, and the prestige of Charles "Martel," or "the Hammer," as he came to be called after his victory, was greatly increased.

When Charles died in 741, he left part of the territory he controlled to a son who soon abdicated and went into a monastery, and the other half to his son Pepin, called "the Short." (There was a shadowy Merovingian king somewhere in the background, but, as usual, he was busy doing nothing.) Such was the prestige enjoyed by the heir of Charles Martel that once Pepin had put down the customary rebellions — a change of regime always seemed to evoke revolts among the Franks — he was left in full control of the realm of Francia, although he was still only a mayor of the palace.

Pepin the Short reunites the kingdom under God
Pepin held a view of his position that must have seemed radical to his contemporaries. Frankish kings and other rulers had always regarded the lands they governed as their personal possessions, to be used to enhance their own wealth and prestige. Pepin, however,

had been educated by Catholic monks and began to think differently. "To us," he said, "the Lord hath entrusted the care of government." The concept that rulership is a sacred trust, bestowed by God on a man who would act as his steward, implies a wholly new theory of political responsibility. With this principle, Pepin had taken a giant step away from tribal chiefdom and toward Catholic monarchy.

He took another step in 751, when he sent envoys to Pope Zacharias to pose a moral question to the highest authority in the Church: was it right that a man who exercised no political power should have the title of king? The pope replied in the negative. The last Merovingian was thereupon packed off to a monastery, where he died the following year, and Pepin the Short, anointed by St. Boniface in what was to become a sacred custom of the kings of France, was now King Pepin.

From then until his death in 768, Pepin worked tirelessly for both his kingdom and the Church. Pope Stephen II came to Francia in 754 to meet with the king and anoint him, giving him and his sons Roman titles formerly held only by the Eastern emperor's representative. Pepin worked with Boniface against corruption among the clergy and sent help to Rome to deliver the pope from the aggression of the Lombard invaders. (These latecomers, a Germanic tribe apparently plodding along at the tail end of the invasions that had toppled Rome, were in the process of occupying much of the top half of the Italian peninsula. They would be a headache for the papacy and the Eastern Empire for some time to come.) Pepin also enlarged the Papal States by a donation of conquered territory to increase papal security. By 759, the last remnants of the Muslim presence in the far south of Gaul were eliminated, and the Franks at last controlled their Mediterranean coast. There are even small signs that Pepin tried to elevate

Frankish culture: he requested books from the pope in Greek. In all, he was a good and worthy king, a fit predecessor to his even greater son.

Enter Charles the Great

When he died in 768, Pepin left his kingdom to his two sons, Carloman and Charles. Three years later, Carloman died suddenly (the same year the weak and scandal-ridden Pope Stephen IV was succeeded by the courageous Hadrian I, whose reign would be intertwined with Charlemagne's), and at the age of twenty-nine, Charles was left as sole king.

Unlike his short father, Charles was quite tall and certainly in excellent physical condition. This is amply demonstrated by the staggering amount of fighting he had to do in order to protect his realm, leading dozens of campaigns in person and directing many others. His keen intelligence, military talent, piety, energy, and devotion to the Church mark him one of the greatest Western rulers of all time.

His military campaigns — something like sixty, half of which he led in person — were impressive on their own. He fought the enemies of his kingdom on all fronts: the turbulent, treaty-breaking Saxons on the northeast, the savage Avars in the east, the Muslims and Basques in the south. The cause of the Church was his, so he defended the papacy against its enemies. It was, in fact, one of his first moves as king to protect Pope Hadrian (later on it would be Leo III) from the Lombards. A campaign against the Muslims across the Pyrenees was one of the few that turned sour; Charlemagne was forced into a tragic retreat back over the mountains, immortalized in *The Song of Roland*.

But Charles was much more than a successful field general. Under his wise administration and ingenious organization, the land of the Franks became truly united. Soon it would be proper to speak, not of a kingdom, but of an empire; for areas that had never been part of the Frankish kingdom were either conquered by Charlemagne or became his tributaries. Some of the peoples with whom he had to cope are hardly remembered now, but they were the subjects of fearful legends in their day.

One of these peoples was the Avars, from what is now Hungary. These nomads have been compared to the Huns for their fierceness and destructive behavior. In Eastern Europe they attacked the Slavs and the Germans, but made a great mistake when they pushed their luck and attacked Bavaria, which had become allied with Charles. The king repulsed them, and when the Avars were then attacked by a Slav army and a bit later by Italians, they were utterly defeated. They disappeared as a people, their remnants apparently melting into the other eastern populations, leaving behind in Hungary a treasure trove that was recently excavated and put on display. It reveals the loot gathered by the Avars in their heyday from as far east as Byzantine territory, as well as more primitive objects — often with the horse motif typical of steppe nomads. Had not Charlemagne stopped them, Western Europe might have been in for another session with these would-be imitators of Attila.

For all these areas, he organized an efficient governmental structure, allowing the various peoples he ruled to keep their own law codes, although he insisted that some essential legal principles be inserted into all of them. Before Charlemagne, tribal laws were often transmitted orally, so Charles had them transcribed; he then revised them or added to them while leaving their particular character intact. Thus Christian principles appeared in the capitularies he issued for the different tribes. There were requirements that the local authorities dispense justice through agents they could trust,

that the poor not be oppressed, that criminals be brought to judgment. The revised code for the Saxons, a violent and recently
converted people, emphasized the renunciation of their pagan
past. Worship of trees and other natural things was forbidden, as
were human sacrifice, burning of churches, and failure to baptize
children.

Charlemagne issued numerous other laws, dealing with everything from monetary regulations to treatment of peasants, to taxes
and questions of business and trade. Still others dealt with Church
affairs. In 802, he issued a capitulary addressing monastic life, re-
quiring that monks "entirely shun drunkenness and feasting, because it is known to all that from these men are especially polluted
by lust." He expresses concern at reports of immorality in monasteries — particularly the "most pernicious rumor" that "some of
the monks are understood to be sodomites" — and vows that "if
any such report shall have come to our ears in the future, we shall
inflict such a penalty, not only on the guilty but also on those who
have consented to such deeds, that no Christian who shall have
heard of it will ever dare in the future to perpetrate such acts."
Would that it had turned out that way.

The royal civil service was international, not exclusively Frankish; he looked for talented men from all over the empire, not just
from among his own people or from the upper classes. He kept
tabs on the far reaches of his realm by appointing men whose loyalty he could trust — the *missi dominici* — to check on conditions
throughout the empire and report back to him.

A rebirth of learning

The pious Charlemagne, who attended daily Mass and vespers,
cared greatly for the welfare of the Church, the purity of clerical
morals, and especially, it seems, the education of the clergy. A

letter he wrote (or dictated, rather, for oddly enough the great king, who could speak two or three languages and seems to have read voraciously, could not write) to Abbot Baugulf of Fulda illustrates his belief that the Church's future was tied to education:

> [T]he bishoprics and monasteries entrusted by the favor of Christ to our control . . . ought also to be zealous in teaching those who by the gift of God are able to learn, according to the capacity of each individual, so that just as the observance of the rule imparts order and grace to honesty of morals, so also zeal in teaching and learning may do the same for sentences, so that those who desire to please God by living rightly should not neglect to please Him also by speaking correctly. . . . For although correct conduct may be better than knowledge, knowledge precedes conduct.[4]

The king refers to letters he has received from various monasteries, in which could be found "both correct thoughts and uncouth expressions" (I can't help thinking of student papers here) and expresses a concern that "as the skill in writing was less, so also the wisdom for understanding the Holy Scriptures might be much less than it rightly ought to be. And we all know well that, although errors of speech are dangerous, far more dangerous are errors of the understanding."

He then expresses a desire — or a command — for the improvement of education in the monasteries, choosing "such men . . . as have both the will and the ability to learn and a desire to instruct others." This is the origin of the great Carolingian Renaissance.

Thus, with his typical energy, Charles set about to promote education and learning within his empire. It happened that one Alcuin of York, a middle-aged English scholar and schoolmaster on his way home from Rome, met Charlemagne at Parma in Italy.

He seems to have known of the king's interest in learning and admired his efforts, and they conversed at length. One thing led to another, and suddenly Alcuin found himself in charge of the new school set up in Charlemagne's palace at Aachen, his capital. It was not what Alcuin had planned for his later years, but he threw himself into the work with a will and began to set up courses and assemble faculty from all over Europe. The books they used were already there, waiting in monastery libraries where they had been copied for centuries, although gradually their meaning had been lost. (Alcuin was to have yet a third career in his old age, when he thought he was retiring to monastic life: he became a great librarian and collector of precious books. Somehow scholars never manage to quit work.)

Alcuin and his scholars slowly became acquainted with the treasures of learning contained in their books, an enterprise that took persistence, intelligence, and systematic effort. The vocabulary of Classical Latin had to be mastered; the terms and principles of unfamiliar sciences had to be grasped; the definitions of theological terms had to be puzzled out and pondered. It was a Herculean task, and it was not all accomplished within the brief period of Charlemagne's version of Camelot.

Yet we must realize what a great thing this was, a ray of light in a cultural darkness. All through the previous centuries, the cultural heritage of Rome — once so vibrant in Gaul, Spain, England, and throughout the Roman Empire — had been submerged in the tide of barbarian invasion. Classical and sacred learning survived in pockets here and there, and with individual scholars: Boethius and Cassiodorus in Italy, St. Bede in England are some of them. By the sixth and seventh centuries, however, even those who passed for educated men demonstrate a very low level of literacy.

St. Gregory of Tours, chronicler of the Merovingians, knew his limitations and humbly apologized for them:

I am afraid that when I start writing without education in rhetoric and grammar, cultured people will say, "You country bumpkin all untrained, do you expect your name to appear among writers? Do you expect this work to be accepted by experienced men, you who cannot distinguish between nouns, who often mix up your genders, who misplace your prepositions, and confuse the ablative with the accusative? You will look like a clumsy ox in a wrestling-school, like a crow among the doves!"

Now there was, for the first time since the fall of Rome, a coordinated, empire-wide onslaught on ignorance, an organized campaign to recover the wisdom of the past and teach its nearly lost skills. The palace school taught both boys and girls, and elementary schools (also teaching both sexes, it seems) were set up all over the king's lands. Above all, Charles was mindful of his responsibilities for the spiritual welfare of his people, and he cared intensely about the religious instruction they were given. In many areas, this was either nonexistent or of very poor quality. There had been clerical and monastic schools in the sixth century, but they had mostly perished in the upheavals of the eighth century. In 794, a local council obeyed the king's wishes by urging bishops to provide instruction to their clergy. Monasteries were to do the same. Charlemagne himself took courses in the palace school and taught subjects on which he was knowledgeable. It was a heady experience for the little band of scholars, no longer reading the classics and learning in solitude, but sharing the experience with friends and progressing in their understanding of almost-lost learning.

Even the art of writing made great strides with the invention of Carolingian Minuscule — a new way of forming letters and separating words that was much easier to read, and would form the basis for modern Western script. Features that we take for granted in writing and printing — clear formation of letters, without unnecessary frills, distinction between capitals and lowercase letters, separation between words — were innovations from Charlemagne's time. Compared with some late Roman manuscripts, written all in capitals, with no spaces between words, the Carolingian Minuscule is a marvel of clarity and a great contribution to the art of writing. The binding and illumination of books, the composition of poems, elegant letters, histories, works in theology and literature all flourished; not all Carolingian works are masterpieces, but they represent a milestone in Western cultural revival. Charlemagne was even interested in the old German tales passed down in the vernacular, which he wanted to have written down and preserved (he also seems to have fostered a similar project in his Romance or French-speaking lands, but these works have been lost). If for nothing else — and there *is* so much else — Charles would deserve the title of "the Great" for his renaissance alone.

Birth of a new empire: Christendom

The crowning glory of Charles's reign occurred when it still had fourteen years to go. Well before the year 800, it was clear to many astute observers that Charlemagne was something new in the history of the West; one of them called him "the father of Europe." He was much greater than a mere king, and indeed the territory he controlled approximated the old Western Roman Empire (minus Spain). So it was that the thought occurred to many of the clerical and lay notables who accompanied Charles to Rome for Christmas, in the year 800, that he should have the title of emperor. Pope Leo certainly agreed, for he crowned Charlemagne emperor on Christmas Day in St. Peter's.

There are conflicting accounts of exactly whose idea it was, whether Charles was surprised, or whether he was even pleased with the coronation, but what's important is that it was done. For the first time since the collapse of Roman power in the West, there was someone to whom the peoples of Europe could look as the one political authority, sanctioned by the Church, and uniting most of the European continent. The Church had the guarantee of a more powerful protector than the various barbarian kings of the past; a growing Church and a well-governed state would now cooperate in promoting the spiritual and temporal welfare of Christians.

Most important, neither sphere would dominate the other. In the late fifth century, Pope St. Gelasius had foreseen the danger that the newly Christian Roman Empire of his day might treat the Church as one of the departments of the state, and this caesaro-papism was in fact practiced in Byzantium. But in the West, a balance — a delicate one, occasionally upset by one party or the other — would be kept from the time of Charlemagne's crowning. So, too, would the tradition of popes crowning the emperors of what would come to be called, in the following century, the Roman Empire.

And so Western Christendom began to take definite shape, its peoples all part of a great Christian commonwealth. Its center was no longer the Mediterranean but the north of Europe, far from the reach of the Muslim raids that threatened even Rome. Its great waterway would be the Atlantic. The concept of the Catholic monarch as defender of the Church and promoter of Christianity, the idea of morally responsible kingship, the cooperation of Church and state, each in its own sphere, were all part of the new Catholic world that had come into being under Charlemagne.

The Coronation of Charlemagne

That unique thing known as Western Civilization was born of three elements: Christianity, Classical culture, and the traditions of the peoples of Europe. These have formed our heritage for so long that we often do not see them as things that might never have come together at all. Following the fall of Rome, Catholicism might have remained a weak and geographically limited religion, hemmed in by northern barbarians, southern Muslims, and eastern schismatics. The few cultural lights that flickered during the Dark Ages might well have died out, and ignorance triumphed among the faithful. That things turned out quite otherwise was due to God's providence in raising up his champions, the Franks. Clovis, Pepin, and Charles Martel had begun the creation and defense of the Christendom of Europe, but it was Charlemagne who promoted the fusion of Catholic, Roman, and Germanic creativity that became our permanent heritage. So strong were the foundations on which he built that the disasters of the late ninth and tenth centuries could not destroy them, and on the other side of the year 1000, a yet more glorious Europe would emerge, one with a mission that would affect the whole world.

910 AD

The Founding of Cluny and the Revival of Religious Life

It was the early tenth century, and Europe was under attack. For over fifty years the peoples of Europe had been struggling to fend off the third wave of invasions to hit them since the fall of Rome. The first wave had brought the Germans and the Huns; the second, the Muslims. This time, the danger came from the northwest with the Vikings, and from the east with the Magyars. Already before Charlemagne's death, Danish raiders had pillaged the north coasts, although (fortunately for the empire, which had no fleet) without mounting a sustained, large-scale attack. Since then, conditions in Europe had deteriorated in almost every way. Charlemagne's empire had passed from the weak rule of his son to his three grandsons, among whom it was divided according to Frankish custom. One took the western part, the future France, and one the eastern area that would become Germany. That left the "Middle Kingdom" for the third son, a long strip with shifting borders that ran down the middle of Europe and would be fought over by its neighbors well into the twentieth century.

The Viking raids had begun in earnest by the mid-ninth century and continued into the tenth, devastating Europe. These pagan marauders had been used to raiding and returning home again with booty and slaves, but for unknown reasons they now began to settle in some of the areas they had previously merely plundered. ("Merely plundered" is putting it mildly; particularly in Ireland and coastal England they wreaked terrible havoc, destroying towns, monasteries, and libraries full of precious books, and taking numerous slaves.) Pouring down the river systems of Eastern Europe, some Vikings founded what would become the first Russian state at Kiev. Others went the other way, across the Atlantic to Iceland, which they colonized, and on to Greenland and probably to North America. Still more plundered the Atlantic coastline, following the rivers to cities such as Paris, or sailing around Spain into the Mediterranean to attack targets there.

People within their reach fled inland in terror to get away from them, often to meet an even worse fate: the Magyars. This group of fierce pagan nomads from the steppes struck Europe from the east in the late ninth century. They were called Hungarians because they were thought to be related to the dreaded Huns of the fifth century, although they actually were not. There were some similarities, however. The Magyars rode fast steppe horses and were skilled bowmen, appearing and disappearing swiftly and unpredictably before warnings could be issued. From their camp in Pannonia in modern Hungary, they penetrated deep into Western Europe, killing and looting as they went. All the while Muslim fleets were mounting new attacks on the Mediterranean coasts.

Dangers for the Church

The situation in the Church mirrored the chaos in society, while in Rome the interference of the quarreling heirs of Charlemagne in papal politics, along with the meddling of powerful Italian factions, dragged down the papacy even as friction with the Church in Byzantium increased. Amid all this turmoil, the influence of laymen over the affairs of the Church grew ever greater. To a great extent, this was connected with the threats Europe was facing all around. In the face of invasion and the collapse of effective political power, new arrangements had come to exist in the former Carolingian Empire. It was no longer the emperor to whom people looked for protection, but the nearest fighting landlord. If those seeking protection were peasants, they would be willing to live on the lord's land and farm it for him, keeping only what they needed for themselves and living under his protection. Clergy, too, might seek such protection, which could also mean ceding control of their property and tolerating the interference of laymen in the running of local Church affairs. As for landless fighting men, they would ally themselves with a more powerful lord in return for a piece of land or another benefit. Thus the system known as feudalism or manorialism emerged from the ruins of the empire of Charles the Great as a means of meeting the needs of a very bleak time. For the Church, it marked the humble beginnings of what would become a centuries-long struggle against domination by temporal powers.

A number of ills beset the Church during this period, apart from the precarious situation in Rome. Among the Franks, and thus throughout the former Carolingian Empire, bishops and other ecclesiastical officials had usually come from noble families and often possessed large properties. Their interests as leaders of the Church often coincided with their temporal interests. In a state based on Catholic principles, as Charlemagne's was, this was probably not a serious problem, but it was soon to become one.

One danger was that temporal goods and goals could engender worldliness and laxity among the clergy; another was that the lands and wealth of the Church would tempt secular lords to try to take them over. Monasteries became enmeshed in the feudal system and found their abbots being appointed by local political leaders or, at a higher level, by kings. The practice of simony — the buying and selling of Church positions — was rife, with prominent bishops and abbots paying large sums to feudal lords for appointment to desirable posts. The ignorance of the clergy increased with lay control and the disorders of the times, and so did clerical immorality. It was not unusual for priests to be "married," more or less openly, or to have concubines — female or male.

Even decent monastic communities could be changed for the worse by the raids. Their scattered members had to fend for themselves, fighting for their very survival. When at last — or if — the survivors reassembled, they were not the monks they had been. The recovery of discipline, asceticism, and the spirit of their rule had become too difficult, if not actually uncongenial, to men grown used to other ways. The great spiritual edifice of the Benedictine Rule, created by St. Benedict in the sixth century and used in most of the monasteries scattered throughout Europe, was no longer in force at religious houses, either through ignorance or because of corruption. Those few devout souls, clerical and lay, who realized how bad things had become saw no means of combating the corruption that existed on such a vast and many-faceted scale. It hardly seemed like a time for great spiritual renewal to take seed.

The miracle

Who would have expected, then, what was to follow? In the year 910, while religious life was at a nadir and Magyars and Vikings were sowing panic and disorder among the peoples of the West, a monastery was founded in Burgundy. Nothing exceptional about that, but what *was* surprising — divinely surprising, one could say — was first, that a layman had founded it, from purely spiritual motives; and second, that after founding it, he thereupon renounced all control over it. This was almost unprecedented. At that time, monastic houses were frequently situated on the extensive and desirable family lands of an early abbot of noble family. They had long been known for their pioneering agricultural techniques, which, combined with the discipline and industry of the monks, made many of them quite prosperous. Furthermore, pious (or repentant) laymen were always leaving bequests in their wills to the monasteries, in the form of land, endowment funds, buildings, valuable sacred objects, or useful equipment. All this increased their net value. If you founded a monastery in those days, then, you wanted your money's worth, and not just spiritually!

The duke and the abbot

This new monastery founded in 910, however, found itself completely free of lay control. This, of course, would count for very little if the abbot and monks were like too many other abbots and monks of the day, looking for an easy, safe, and pleasurable life — profitable too, perhaps — in a monastic house. But there was a third divine surprise: the first abbot of this monastery was a saint. Not only was he a saint, but he came to be succeeded by a long line of saintly abbots, all of them canonized or beatified. This is the story of Cluny.

Desiring to employ, in a manner useful for my soul, the goods God has given me, I thought I could not do better than to win for myself the friendship of the poor. In order that this work might be perpetual, I wished to maintain at my expense a community of monks. I therefore give, for the love of God and of our Lord Jesus Christ, to the holy Apostles Peter and Paul, from my own domain, the land of

Cluny. . . . I give it for the soul of my lord, King Eudes, and for the souls of my parents and servants. . . .

These monks and all these goods will be under the authority of the abbot Berno as long as he shall live; but after his death, the religious will have the power to elect as abbot, according to the rule of St. Benedict, whomever they please, without the prevention of regular election by any authority. . . .

From this day, they will be neither subject to us, nor to our relatives, nor to the king, nor to any power on earth. No secular prince, no count, no bishop, not even the pope himself — I beg them all in the name of God and of the saints and of the Day of Judgment, not to take over the goods of these servants of God, nor to sell, exchange, or diminish them, or to give them in fief to anyone, and not to impose on them a superior against their will.[5]

This landmark charter, issued September 11, 910, came from a man of whom we know little: William the Pious, Duke of Aquitaine. He had a famous great-grandmother, Dhuoda, who lived in the middle of the previous century and was of the Carolingian aristocracy. Her husband and elder son were executed by King Charles the Bald, who accused them of betraying him, but her second son, Bernard, survived and became the grandfather of William the Pious. In 843 Dhuoda completed her *Handbook*, written for her elder son. Its theme is the behavior of a perfect knight within the feudal system, and it includes practical advice on the reciprocal duties of lords and vassals. Dhuoda's overriding concern, however, is for the spiritual life of her son, to which she relates his worldly duties. She urges him to be "reborn each day in Christ," and "grow always in Christ." The *Handbook* was well known in its time, and it might have been the deep spirituality of his ancestress that helped Duke William II become "the Pious." (William also seems to have had a pious mother, Ermengarde, who founded an abbey in the town of Blesle in Auvergne, around the year 885.)

We sometimes read a date of 909 instead of 910 for the founding of Cluny. Possibly this is merely a much-copied dating error, but it might also refer to the actual negotiations about the new enterprise, which likely occurred for many months prior to September of 910. William had first of all to find monks willing to accept his offer, and as it happened — providentially, no doubt — there was a tiny group in search of just what he had in mind. St. Berno, of a noble Burgundian family, seems to have been a whirlwind of reforming activity all by himself, even before he met the duke. He had first founded, some twenty years before 910, a model monastery on his own property of Gigny and then gone to be a monk of St. Martin's in Autun, where he learned about the practices and spirit of the Benedictines. From there, he went on to restore the monastery of Baume, in the Jura Mountains of what is now Switzerland, a project for which he had obtained funds from the king of Burgundy. His energy and determination next took him to Rome, where he obtained from Pope Formosus a bull allowing the monks of Baume free election of their abbot and exemption from ecclesiastical taxes.

This was already quite a record of achievement. Applicants flocked to his two houses, known to be among the most fervent, and most faithful to the Rule of St. Benedict, in Europe. Soon St. Berno needed still more space, and it must have been about 909 that he thought of asking Duke William for a villa located on his land at Cluny. The following year, William signed the famous charter in the presence of several bishops and many laymen, and the new establishment, housing the monks from both Gigny and Baume, became a reality.

The duke is said in some sources to have been an elderly man then (he died in 918) and might have felt his life drawing to a close in 910. At that date, St. Berno, on the other hand, was just embarking on his historic sixteen-year rule of what would become the greatest monastic foundation of the time.

St. Berno spreads the zeal for reform

The first abbot of Cluny was initially concerned with firmly establishing the provisions of St. Benedict's Rule and the old Benedictine traditions and way of life. Soon Cluny became a model monastery, and even more recruits were drawn by its holy reputation. Donations from admiring laymen came in, too (although the monastery was often hard-pressed to provide for the growing number of monks). Still Berno's work was not finished. Several princes and local lords asked him to take over the rule of monasteries they had founded, or hoped to found. One of them was a vassal of Duke William, who had founded a religious house in 917 and given it the kind of privileges William had given Cluny. The holy abbot had more work than he could accept — literally, since according to the canon law at the time, an abbot was not to control several monasteries at once. It seems that little attention was paid to this provision in practice, and in any case, powerful lords had been accumulating religious houses on their lands for a long time. The best of them perceived the corruption in many of these monasteries and begged St. Berno to take them in hand, canon law or no canon law.

Thus the practice arose of laymen giving over control of monasteries, for long or short periods, to Cluny. A colony of Cluniac monks would then be sent to the other establishments to reform abuses and institute full observance of the Rule. St. Berno's connection with all these houses was merely a personal one; he made no formal arrangements to unify them, and before his death of hard work and old age, he divided the rule of his original houses among some of his close associates.

St. Odo: the greatest religious force of his generation

Berno left the rule of Cluny to St. Odo, who was to govern it for twenty-six years. Under his direction, the Cluniac Reform began to spread beyond its original sphere of Burgundy and Aquitaine in France to almost the whole of Europe. This ascetic and mystic was also a practical man: always on the road, winning over powerful laymen to the cause of reform in their lands, visiting numerous monasteries, and spending time with the monks who were most interested in the reform of their houses. When he departed, he left groups of Cluniacs to carry on the work.

Not all the monasteries were eager to be reformed. There is the interesting example of Fleury, on the Loire River, to which Odo was invited by the count in whose territory it lay. It was one of those communities that had been scattered by Viking attacks and had trouble getting itself together again. It was also dear to Benedictine hearts since it possessed the relics of St. Benedict of Nursia himself. As Odo approached the monastery, he must have been surprised to see monks on the roofs and at the doors armed with weapons. It seems these brethren had had a rough time of it during the Viking raids, and when at length they managed to reassemble in their monastery, they wanted to recover the way of life they had known there before. Just when they were trying to do this, here comes a strange monk on a mission to turn things upside down in the cause of some newfangled "reform." We see their point of view.

After a standoff of three days, St. Odo gave up arguing. Courageously he mounted a donkey and rode up to the main gate. "I come peacefully," he said aloud, "to hurt no one, injure no one, but that I may correct those who are not living according to rule." And such was his evident holiness and charisma that they opened the gates and let him in, and so thoroughly changed did this rebel house become that we consider it the most influential reformed monastery after Cluny itself.

Cluny's allegiance to the Holy See as its overlord drew St. Odo periodically to Rome, where Alberic, Marquis of Spoleto, wielded great influence. Such was the power of Odo's personality that even the marquis joined the cause of reform and gave the abbot authority over several Roman communities and churches. Ironically, or perhaps as a fitting homage to St. Benedict, who lived in a cave there and attracted his first followers, Odo even reformed Subiaco.

A tougher proposition was the Italian abbey of Farfa, near Rome, which Alberic desired St. Odo to reform. When its own abbot had tried to enforce the Rule of St. Benedict there, he was poisoned by two of his monks, one of whom — a man named Campo — then became abbot. He and his accomplice in murder lived in the monastery with their wives and children. In another attempt at cleaning up the place, Campo was expelled, but the new abbot also died of poison. As for Odo, he was never able to get into Farfa, and it was only after his death that the place was finally reformed — by use of military force!

So welcome was the existence of the promising new institution at Cluny that extraordinary provisions were made in its favor. In response to a request from Abbot Odo, Pope John XI issued a papal bull in 931 in which he stated, among other things, "This monastery with all its possessions now and in the future, will be free of any authority by king or bishop, or count or whoever it might be, including, if the case arises, Duke William himself. [This would have been the first William's nephew and successor.] No one, therefore, may presume after your death to propose any person to the monks against their will; but may they have total liberty, without having to consult any authority, to choose a person as their guide according to *regula* of St. Benedict. . . ."

The Church also saw to it that the monastery had sufficient income, guaranteed the monks the right to everything they got from their fields and vines, and even — giving us a glimpse into the varied activities in which the monks were engaged — provided a subsidy for Cluny's hospital. They even had their own coins, "as our son Rudolph, king of the Franks, granted you." Further, the bull continued, "since, as is known, almost all monasteries are now deviating from their calling, we grant that if any monk from any monastery wishes to stop at your community with the sole desire of improving his life and if, evidently, his abbot has neglected to grant what the *regula* establishes . . . you may welcome him; until the life of his monastery is not amended. Thus, we also grant you immunity. . . . [N]o one may assume the right in any way to remove or occupy your property without consulting you."

Effectively put in charge of the whole enterprise of monastic reform, Odo would later obtain similar privileges from Pope Leo VII in 938. By the time he died in 942, he had become, as one historian has put it, "the greatest religious force of his generation."

*More saintly abbots
carry on the work of Cluny*

St. Odo was followed by Bl. Aymard, who continued the work of his great predecessor for most of the eight years he was yet to live. When he began to grow blind, he resigned his office to St. Mayeul. This next abbot and his successors, all saints, were gifted with an extraordinary longevity that provided continuity and harmony to the whole Cluniac enterprise.

St. Mayeul begged in vain not to be made abbot. Once stuck with the position, he served the cause of reform faithfully for forty years. He enjoyed great prestige and influence with emperors — although politely declining Emperor Otto's offer to make him pope — and with other lay rulers, including Hugh Capet, founder of the Capetian dynasty of France. Like Odo, he traveled much, expanding the range of Cluny's influence among the monasteries of Europe and re-reforming houses reformed by St. Odo that had since relapsed. Once, when he and his retinue were ambushed and captured by Muslim raiders in the Alps, his ransom was promptly raised and the local authorities quickly formed an alliance and destroyed the raiding party. His successor wrote of him, "The kings and princes of the earth call him lord and master, and he was truly the prince of monastic religion."

St. Odilo, Odo's successor, ruled even longer than he had: from 994 to 1048. During his term of office, Cluny reached perhaps the height of its power and influence. Odilo was a man of small stature and great heart. While enforcing discipline, he was understanding of human weakness. "If I must be damned," he said, "I would rather be damned because of my mercy than because of my severity." A traveler like his predecessors, and acquainted with the political powers of the day, he also corresponded with kings he was unable to visit personally, such as St. Stephen, the first Catholic king of Hungary. And during his time, parallel reforms, most inspired by his example, were well underway in Germany and England.

Previously, the bond among reformed monasteries and Cluny had been one of personal obedience to the Abbot of Cluny. Under St. Odilo, this loose association came closer to becoming a new institution: an actual religious order or congregation. The affiliated houses were ruled by priors, who, in turn, owed obedience to the abbot of Cluny. In this way they were able to counteract a danger inherent in the original Benedictine organization. Autonomous houses, like the first Benedictine monasteries, were often isolated and vulnerable to lay interference in troubled times. If they became lax and corrupt, there was no higher authority with regular supervision over them. When the Cluniac system corrected this deficiency, it both strengthened the general reform movement and created a powerful and united organism at the service of the Church in the following period.

St. Odilo was succeeded — in a line that must be unique in history, given the average lifespan of the era — by yet another long-lived saint. St. Hugh was the sixth of the saintly abbots and reigned for nearly sixty years, until 1109. The order enjoyed perhaps the pinnacle of its prestige in his time, and he helped spread it to areas that had not known it earlier. England and Spain now had communities of Cluniac monks. It was also Hugh who began, in 1088, the building of the great and famous church known as Cluny III (because it was the third church of the monastery, replacing earlier structures). It was one of the greatest churches of the Middle Ages, although we know it only from archaeological evidence and contemporary records. It is a melancholy fact that both the church and the other buildings of Cluny have almost completely disappeared.

The Cluniac movement sets the
stage for Church-wide renewal

Cluny's success required the cooperation of so many disparate elements, from laymen demanding moral reform of the clergy, to kings encouraging it, to popes implementing it, that its final cohesion and triumph appear as a miracle of grace. The Cluniacs had no such grand scheme in mind when they first dedicated themselves heart and soul to leading pure monastic lives and escaping the corrupting influence of secular control. Their concern with purity of life was an implicit condemnation of clerical immorality, but it would be bishops, preachers, and popes who would actively campaign against the sins of fornication and pederasty among the clergy. Likewise, although Cluny was the first monastery to remove itself from lay control, active resistance to lay investiture would be carried out later, at higher levels. The great movement for reform of both Church and society would not reach its climax for a century, but Cluny set it all in motion. It would, in fact, be a man who had lived and studied at Cluny, Hildebrand, who as Pope St. Gregory VII would bring the reform movement to fruition and spread it throughout the Church.

It is easy to follow the line of progress, once it had all happened, from the pious project of Duke William in 910 to the Gregorian triumph at the end of the following century. Yet even during the great period known to historians as "the Gregorian Epoch," nothing was certain and progress was far from following a consistent upward road. False starts, beginnings that led nowhere, and turns for the worse would all be part of the long, weary struggle. It was accomplished in the end, however, and its genesis was the inspiration and holiness of Cluny.

1000 AD

Gateway to the Church's Most Glorious Age

The historian Anselm of Liege reports how the German King Otto was on campaign with his army in 968, accompanied by a bishop, when the sunlight began to disappear and darkness spread over the earth. Immediately the tough warriors panicked and, wailing about the coming of the Last Judgment, they tried to hide themselves wherever they could — even in barrels and under their carts. Only the bishop was unperturbed, since he knew something of astronomy, and promised the cowering men that the sun would shortly return!

I know of no modern historian who accepts the old myth of a widespread expectation that the end of the world was at hand as the end of the first millennium approached. The documents of the time simply do not support that thesis.

But there is undeniably a measure of fear and pessimism evident in tenth-century writings — only too well founded, given the devastating battles, raids, and famines of the time. For despite the emergence of Cluny, the state of Christendom had been spiraling downward throughout the 900s in almost every way. The chaos brought by the relentless barbarian raids had disrupted daily life, government, agriculture, education, and religion in most of Europe. Some wrote of comets and other portents of dire things to come; there seems also to have been increased interest in the subject of the anti-Christ.

And yet, thanks to the work of the Carolingian Renaissance, learning and culture were still being passed on, despite the obstacles, so the age was not as dark as the period immediately following the fall of Rome. And after the turn of the millennium, there are a few hints of a different spirit abroad. Thietmar of Merseburg wrote, about 1013, that "a morning dawned radiant on the world," and the often somber Raoul Glaber, recorder of dark portents, wrote about 1030 that "it seemed as if the world, shaking itself and casting off its old age, was putting on, here, there, and everywhere, the pure white robe of churches." This is a significant remark. These churches were not the mean wooden structures of the time of upheaval, when there were neither the resources for nor a point to building anything better because it was likely to be destroyed in the next invasion. These tall, strong churches of white stone, gleaming in the sun and visible for miles around, were the symbol of a great change, harbingers of a new and glorious age to come.

The material roots of
a new Catholic culture

Two material factors underlay what would become the civilization of the High Middle Ages: the cessation of barbarian invasions (with the exception of the Muslim raids in the south) and an agricultural revolution that was one of the turning points of European economic history. Since a minimum level of material prosperity seems to be necessary for any cultural flowering (men living at subsistence level have neither time nor means for creativity), economic improvement was necessary if European civilization was to pick up the pieces it had dropped during the last century.

As with so many things that came to full fruition in the twelfth and thirteenth centuries, the foundations of the agricultural revolution had been laid in the time of Charlemagne. During and following his reign, the practice of allowing part of the farmland to lie fallow, meaning that no crops would be sown in it, began; this increased crop yields when the "fallow" was sown the following year. Some Roman technology had been rediscovered, such as the waterwheel, and inventions like the heavy plow and the horse-collar made cultivation of heavy northern soil easier. Charlemagne had encouraged trade within his empire and even beyond, thus fostering the growth of a merchant class that further stimulated economic activity. By the mid-eleventh century, fairs were being held in many parts of Europe, to which craftsmen and merchants could bring their wares (and the news of the day) and exchange them for other products. Villages grew larger, as craftsmen flourished and merchants required warehouse space, and at last the people of Europe began to experience true urban life for the first time since the fall of Rome. Towns grew into real cities, and these, in turn, became the centers for cathedrals, universities, hospitals, and increasingly efficient royal governments.

Of course, the flourishing of Christendom did not take place overnight. Despite agricultural progress, nearly half the years in the eleventh century were years of famine. The thoroughgoing reform of the Church and its liberation from secular control would take most of the century to achieve. The news from the East was bad, as the Arab conquerors of much of the Byzantine Empire, including the Holy Land, were replaced by the equally militant Seljuk Turks. Not until the end of the century, with the First Crusade in 1095, would Europe be able to mount a great military expedition against the Muslims. Nonetheless, despite the shadows that are part of any period in history, however glorious it may be, Christendom after the year 1000 launched into its greatest age.

An abundance of blessings

During the three centuries that followed, the climate continued to be generally favorable to agricultural production. (Except for relatively recent centuries, climatic conditions and changes of the past are poorly understood. There are indications, however, that European weather was warmer during the Early and High Middle Ages than it was later on. In the thirteenth century, for instance, grapes were grown in England and grain in most of Norway; a century later, those crops could no longer be produced in those countries.)

Western Europe continued free of any major outside invasion, Church reform achieved one goal after another, and the countries of Europe experienced stronger and more efficient government than they had known for centuries, often with saints for rulers. Learning and the arts began to flourish to a degree unknown since, perhaps, the fifth century BC in Athens. The first new architectural style in seven hundred years — the Gothic — is evidence of great originality in the culture of the Middle Ages, and it is paralleled in the intellectual sphere by the sublime works of scholastic philosophers such as St. Thomas Aquinas and St. Bonaventure. Science, the visual arts, music, political thought, and spirituality flourished as never before between the years 1000 and 1300.

A truly Catholic culture

The inspiration for this period of creativity and achievement was the Faith. The principles that shaped politics, economics, philosophy, literature, and other cultural forms, the attitudes of men toward everything in life — all derived from Catholicism. This is certainly not to say that all medieval Catholics were saints; they were sinners like the rest of us, and there were plenty of prominent villains around, as there always are. But unlike in our day, most sinners and villains acknowledged that that is what they *were*. Except in the cases of some of the more extreme heretics, they did not try to pretend they were really some new kind of saint. In the High Middle Ages, Catholic doctrine and spirituality informed all of public and private life to a greater extent than ever before or since. It was the closest we have ever come to the visible reign of Christ the King on earth.

The kings of the West

As for the earthly kings of Christendom in this age, at the time of the new millennium, the rulers of the three main Western states of England, France, and Germany were all struggling to assert their authority within their realms and defend them from outside attack. England continued to experience Viking raids in the north and was taken over after the death of King St. Edward the Confessor (apparently according to his wishes) by Northmen who had settled in Normandy, in the west of France, and had there become both civilized and Catholic. William of Normandy, now William I of England, made his new kingdom a strong feudal state in which he encouraged Church reforms.

The line of Charlemagne gave way, in both France and Germany, to new dynasties with very different goals. In the eleventh century, the French kings had controlled only the area immediately around Paris. By the mid-thirteenth century, their patient assertion of their authority over a larger and larger sphere had paid off, and France was the most prosperous, powerful, and cultured kingdom of the West, with one of the greatest of the royal saints — Louis IX — for its king.

The German kings, on the other hand, pursued three unrealistic goals that they were destined not to achieve. They wanted to gain power over the independent barons of Germany, they wanted to control the influential Church, and they wanted to incorporate Italy, including Rome, into their Holy Roman Empire. Had they stayed home, they might well have developed the sort of nation-state the English and French kings had achieved. As soon as they left Germany to fight the Italians, however, as they routinely did during the eleventh, twelfth, and thirteenth centuries, revolt broke out in Germany. Whenever they hurried back across the Alps to deal with that, the Italians threw off German rule. And their constant attempts to take over the Church, including trying to control papal elections, increasingly outraged both clerical and lay opinion, and provided ammunition for the ecclesial reformers who would prove their greatest antagonists, as we shall see.

Guardians of the heavenly kingdom: the popes

The Catholic inspiration of medieval culture and its tremendous achievements could be maintained only by the ceaseless vigilance of the institutional Church. Here we rejoin the reformers of the previous chapter (for it is a fact that fallible human beings are in constant need of reform). The movement inspired, to a large extent, by the holy influence of Cluny, was one part of the drive to eliminate evil within the Church, but it was not the whole of it. Dedicated monks could achieve noble goals — purity of life, fidelity to the Rule, freedom from lay control — within religious houses and exert a beneficial influence on lay society, but some of the worst abuses of the time were beyond their reach. Simony, the buying and selling of clerical offices, had to be dealt with by popes, especially since bishops could often be the most visible and scandalous offenders. Similarly, the problem of kings

meddling in Church affairs, including the appointing and depos-
ing of popes, could be confronted only at the papal level.

Pope St. Leo IX: reform must come from the top!
One of the landmarks of the papal reform movement occurred
in the mid-eleventh century with the pontificate of Pope St. Leo
IX. A great admirer of Cluny, he had tried to introduce Cluniac
principles into his diocese when he was Bishop Bruno of Toul.
When the papal throne became vacant in 1049, Emperor Henry
III followed long-standing practice by appointing Bruno pope,
with the advice of the German clergy.

Now, this Henry was himself a saintly man, who strenuously
pursued Church reform at all levels. He supported the Cluniac reform and is said to have once tried to become a monk, only to have
the abbot command him under obedience to go on ruling his
country. Henry's ancestors had become involved over the centuries in papal affairs because the influence of corrupt factions in
Rome had made free papal elections impossible. Imperial support
had been crucial to the survival of several pontificates, and the emperors had often appointed and maintained holy and competent
men on the papal throne. St. Henry thus saw nothing wrong in appointing his saintly relative pope; he certainly did not do it from
any political motive, and the German clergy had agreed with him.

St. Leo, however, unlike most of his predecessors, refused to
consider himself pope until he had been duly elected by the Roman clergy and people, according to the ancient custom. According to one account, during a visit he made to Cluny, he received
advice on this question from the prior, Hildebrand, the future
Gregory VII. Leo's insistence on this customary Roman election
gave impetus to the movement that, by the end of the century,
would see papal elections vested in the College of Cardinals and

removed from imperial control. Duly elected in Rome in 1049, Leo then set out to work with all his strength for the cause of reform — this time starting not at the bottom with monks and priests, but at the top: with the bishops. After calling a council in Rome that condemned simony in no uncertain terms, he took the campaign on the road; most of his brief pontificate, in fact, would be spent traveling and holding local reforming councils.

The first of these took place at Reims later in the year 1049, on the day when the French were honoring the great St. Remigius, who had baptized Clovis. Leo appeared, bearing the remains of the great saint on his shoulders and, in a dramatic historical moment, demanded that all the bishops present swear in the presence of St. Remigius that they had not paid money for their offices. Consternation! There were bishops present from Germany, France, England, and elsewhere, and they were taken off guard. Some actually (and speedily) left the council, while others confessed and were forgiven by the Holy Father, although they were also given penances to perform. This was the beginning of the elimination of the great evil of simony from the Church, and Leo pursued the simoniacs all over Europe until he died in 1054. By the time his papacy ended, the practice of simony was far less common than it had been, and after the pontificate of Pope St. Gregory VII, two decades later, simony was a spent force.

Not so successful was Leo's attempt to reconcile the Greek Church with Rome; he unfortunately sent to Constantinople a very undiplomatic cardinal, Humbert of Silva Candida, who so irritated the Greeks during their negotiations that the formal existence of the Greek Schism is dated from his ill-fated visit in 1054 — the year of Leo's death. Leo's continued intervention might yet have been able to save the situation; however, we will never know because, in another ill-fated move later that same year, he led an army against the Normans of southern Italy. These descendants of the Vikings had seized papal territory that Leo, a former soldier, was determined they should not have. He failed in this enterprise, was captured, and died soon after his release.

Pope St. Gregory VII: the climax of reform

The eleventh-century pope whose name has been given to the whole reform movement — it is often known as "the Gregorian Reform" — was the great Pope St. Gregory VII, formerly Hildebrand, advisor to previous popes, diplomat, and saint. He seems to have spent some time as a monk at Cluny, and certainly espoused Cluniac resistance to moral corruption and lay control of the Church. His reign, which began in 1073, included at least one major theological controversy, on the nature of Transubstantiation, and continued mobilization of opinion and punitive measures against clerical immorality and simony. He maintained relations with most of the nations of Europe and even with at least one Muslim ruler in Africa, where he managed to install and maintain two or three bishops. It was during his reign also that St. Bruno founded the new Carthusian Order, destined for a great and holy future.

Gregory worked ceaselessly against the evils of his time, and a letter he wrote to St. Hugh of Cluny early in 1075 reveals how hard the struggle was for him

> If it were possible, I would like to make you feel all the anguish that assails my soul, because I am worn out every day. . . . Your fraternal love would move you then to ask of God that the all-powerful Lord Jesus might deign to give me His hand — to me, miserable one — and deliver me from my troubles. For a long time I have been asking Him either to take

my life or to render me useful to our Mother, Holy Church,
yet He has neither rescued me from my afflictions nor allowed me to render to Holy Church the service I desire to
give her.[6]

Gregory then pours out his distress at the schism of the Eastern
Church and the paucity of good bishops and princes in Europe,
and begs the abbot and all the monks of Cluny for their prayers,
which he would surely need: the great crisis of his reign was about
to unfold.

Gregory the controversial

No two historians seem to agree on the goals and personality
of Pope St. Gregory. Even some Catholic historians are either
highly critical of him or at best lukewarm in their praise of what he
accomplished. (One even remarks snidely that, although he is a
canonized saint, he has never had a popular cult. When I read
that, I started praying to him; he is popular with me anyway.)

The point of controversy is whether he went too far in assert-
ing the prerogatives of the papacy over Christian society, including temporal authorities. This is not the place to examine the
question in great detail. Doing justice to St. Gregory requires
studying his actual words in the language in which they were written or spoken, examining exactly what they signified in the theological discourse of the time, and exploring the situations that
prompted them. This is a fundamental requirement for analyzing
any text, and more than one medieval pope has been misunder-
stood by modern historians who fail in this duty, or are actually ignorant of it.

One example of how complicated this can be: a famous list of
principles apparently drawn up by Gregory, known as the *Dictatus*

papae, can be read as an extreme exaltation of papal power over kings, emperors, and all other Catholics. What was it really, though? At least one historian has suggested it was nothing more than notes for an allocution the pope was planning to give to the cardinals. If that were the case, we would need to know whether he actually gave the address in that form — speakers are not irrevocably committed to their lecture notes! Some writings attributed to Gregory are also of questionable authenticity, so merely discovering exactly what he himself had to say can be a daunting task.

Nonetheless, for our purposes, we can look at the basic facts of the case for what they were. The confrontation that overshadowed most of his pontificate was his epic struggle with Emperor Henry IV over the "investing" of clerics by laymen with the symbols of their position. It is a complicated business, and Gregory, notwithstanding the intransigence of which some historians have accused him, was willing to compromise on many points, depending on the circumstances. In an age when high Churchmen were apt to be also landowners, and when, in some countries, they actually administered lands for the state, it was right that the kings should have some say in their territorial functions. The issue, however, went beyond the practical and was for some a matter of principle; some Germans argued that God had given Constantine, and the German emperors who were seen as his successors, rule over both the temporal *and* spiritual spheres of Christian society.

For Gregory, the family of Catholic nations had as its true head the Vicar of Christ. He acknowledged a distinction between the temporal and spiritual realms, but seems to have held that temporal power was not bestowed directly on rulers by God as a divine right. True, God imposed solemn duties upon them, but if they ceased to rule rightly, it was up to the pope to judge them as having failed in their moral obligations; and, if necessary, even declare them deposed and release their subjects from obedience to them.

Thus this issue of investiture was so inextricably immersed in both the spiritual and the temporal spheres, so tangled up with history, custom, good effects, and bad effects, that perhaps only the painful surgery of excommunication and anathema could cut its Gordian knot. This task Gregory had the great burden of undertaking.

The royal adversary

Had the saintly Henry III, who reigned from 1039 to 1056, still been on the German throne, the relationship between the temporal and the spiritual spheres might have been sorted out smoothly. On the other hand, it might not have occurred at all, because no serious conflict would have arisen. It took a nasty character like Henry IV to bring matters to a head. As a child, Henry seems to have been indulged by his widowed mother, who apparently turned a blind eye to his moral faults, lack of self-discipline, and finally, actual depravity of life. He could be unstable and erratic in his actions, and cruel in his treatment of his people. He tyrannized over and deliberately insulted his Saxon subjects, once keeping a delegation waiting all day for an audience while he made jokes at their expense within their hearing, and then dismissed them without allowing them to speak. When at length the Saxons rebelled against his oppression, Henry retaliated by seizing their lands and selling some of the peasants as slaves, using others for forced labor. He was unconcerned with reform. To him, Gregory represented a threat to the German kings' power to interfere in Church affairs and appoint the popes and bishops they wished. Gregory was not even a German, as many of his predecessors had been, but a native of Tuscany and an Italian patriot.

Although the king had accepted the election of Hildebrand 1073 as a *fait accompli*, two years later he called for a new papal election and got the tame German bishops to support him; where-upon Gregory excommunicated him and declared him deposed. This caused the disaffected German princes to rally to the side of the pope, and Henry was desperate to save his throne.

The oft-told tale of Henry at Canossa is a dramatic and a tragic one. Pope Gregory had called for a council to be held at Augsburg in February 1077, at which he would preside and which would deal with the question of the legitimacy of Henry's rule. At the end of December 1076, the pontiff set out on his journey north. Meanwhile, Henry was in a state of great agitation at the thought of what the outcome of the council might be, and how he could forestall a decision that could prove disastrous for him. An idea occurred to him: he would intercept the pope before he left Italy and make his peace with him privately. So he, too, set out in De-cember, going south, and taking his long-suffering and often ne-glected wife and infant son along — perhaps to soften the pope's heart.

The winter of 1076-1077 was one of the most severe in re-corded history, and the mountain passes, dangerous enough even in summer, were perilous in the extreme. Henry's party was held up near Geneva by his mother-in-law, Adelaide, ruler of the terri-tory through which the Germans had to pass. Adelaide disliked Henry for his harsh treatment of his daughter and at first refused to allow him to pass through her lands. Only after he had given up five bishoprics — the revenues of which he had been taking — and his wife had pleaded for him, could he get Adelaide's permis-sion to continue his journey. (At that, it must have been a mixed blessing for him; his mother-in-law, seeing the anxiety and fatigue of her daughter, decided to join the party.) Some of Henry's retinue died in the crossing, and others lost limbs to the terrible cold, but eventually they descended into Italy.

The drama at Canossa

Now, St. Gregory, en route to Germany, was being entertained by his friend and frequent benefactor the Countess Matilda, powerful ruler of Tuscany, who tried unsuccessfully to dissuade him from attempting the dangerous Alpine passes. He had just resolved to continue his journey — on which he might well have perished of the cold, had Henry not interfered — when word came to the countess that Henry and a party of armed men were approaching. Immediately she feared an attack on the pope and took the papal party to her strong fortress of Canossa with its three circles of defensive walls. There he found St. Hugh of Cluny, who had come on other business but was glad to hear of the king's coming, because he was his godfather and still fond of the young monarch.

From his headquarters, Henry sent envoys to the pope with requests for an audience and promises of submission. Gregory merely replied that Augsburg was the place where they would meet. Increasingly frantic, Henry persuaded Matilda and St. Hugh to intercede for him with Gregory; Matilda seems to have agreed out of sympathy for Bertha, Henry's wife, and St. Hugh out of love for his godson. In any case, soon papal permission for Henry to come to the fortress was forthcoming.

Once there, however, the king was surprised to find that he was not immediately received. Indeed, he was kept waiting nearly three days, which he spent barefoot, fasting, and pacing up and down outside the pope's window in penitential garb. He must have been both freezing outwardly and seething inwardly. As for Gregory, he acknowledged later that "all truly wondered at the harshness of our mind, and . . . the cruelty. . . ." He himself had "spent the days and nights in prayer, entreating the Almighty to enlighten us from on high as to what to do in such a serious pass, and what to reserve for the decision of a council."

Gregory must have distrusted the king's motives, but as a priest, he could hardly refuse an outwardly penitent Christian, humbly waiting out there in the snow wearing sackcloth. He finally received the king, who threw himself on the ground before him saying, "Pardon me, Father, pardon me!" With tears in his eyes, Gregory did so. Afterward, the pope celebrated Mass, and after the Consecration, he turned and addressed Henry, holding up the Host. He referred to the false accusations brought against him by Henry and his supporters and declared that he would appeal to God's judgment in the matter: "Let the Body of our Lord Jesus Christ, that we are about to take, be this day a proof of our innocence. We pray the Almighty to dispel all suspicion if we are innocent, and to cause us suddenly to die if we are guilty." Next he summarized the complaints that had been made to him about Henry, and urged him to testify to his innocence in the same way — by the Body of the Lord.

Henry could not do it. He hesitated, visibly distraught, and then requested time for consideration. He consulted his friends, and all agreed he could not commit a sacrilege. Returning to the front of the chapel, he excused himself from communicating on the pretext that so many of his nobility were absent from the scene that it would have no effect on them. "For that purpose, I beg that the test may be postponed to the day of the sitting of the general Diet." Gregory turned around and continued the Mass.

At dinner following the Mass, the pope attempted to engage the king in friendly conversation, meeting only with a cold reserve. Finally he gave him a parting blessing, and Henry went back to Germany. The princes continued their opposition to Gregory. The complex political situation was beyond the pope's control, and when Henry continued to defy the pope on many ecclesiastical issues, he was excommunicated a second time. This time even some of the German bishops who had originally supported the pope went over to the king's side.

The last act

After his second excommunication, Henry took advantage of the confused political situation and divided opinion to set up the excommunicated Archbishop Wilbert (or Guibert) of Ravenna as an anti-pope, "Clement III," and then marched on Rome and installed him in 1080. Most of the cardinals went over to the side of "Clement." As the Germans marched into Italy, the Countess Matilda (an extraordinary woman who as a teenager had twice led her Tuscan troops against a German force attempting to set up an antipope) took the field with her army to try to head them off. Defeated, she took refuge in Canossa, and then, by a clever ruse, succeeded in routing the besieging Germans in a providential thick fog. She then rushed to Rome, while the Germans coming after her laid waste her lands and stole her valuables.

In Rome, she organized the defense of the city, which determined to wait out the German siege that soon began. It continued off and on for over two years, beginning in 1081. The Germans began to suffer from lack of provisions in the winter and malaria in the summer; they were worn out and harassed at night by sorties of Matilda's men from within the city.

Henry, however, succeeded in making contact with Roman traitors, and thanks to their efforts, he entered the city in March 1084; his puppet antipope crowned him "emperor" — the title he had always sought from Gregory.

In this extremity, Pope Gregory received aid from an unlikely quarter: the Normans of southern Italy. These descendants of the Vikings had carved out a state for themselves in Sicily and southern Italy, and had taken over *de facto* possession of lands that were claimed by the Holy See. Although they had become Catholics, they refused to acknowledge papal (or any other) claims over land they had scooped up for themselves. In 1054, Pope St. Leo IX had led an army against the Normans to recover the Duchy of Benevento, northeast of Naples. Part of it seems to have been ceded to the papacy by its duke in the eighth century, and the whole of it was granted to Pope Leo IX by Emperor Henry III in exchange for the bishopric of Bamberg in the early 1050s. When the Normans moved into the area, their Count Drogo assured Leo that he would respect papal suzerainty over Benevento, but when he was assassinated in 1051, the resulting turmoil among the Normans ended with raids on more southern Italian lands. Benevento fell to the Normans in 1053. Pope St. Leo's failed attempt at reconquest came the following year.

Gregory, however, had made an alliance with the Normans in 1080, a few days after Emperor Henry had appointed his antipope. To this alliance they remained faithful, even when the pope had lost many of his former allies. Gregory had sent an urgent message to the Norman leader, Robert Guiscard, when it was clear Rome was about to fall to the Germans. Guiscard rushed to Gregory's aid with his fierce warriors, who drove out Henry's forces from Rome, but then sacked it in their turn — they had no notion of fighting without the reward of rich booty.

Still, Rome was not safe for Gregory; Henry remained too powerful and dangerous. Robert Guiscard, who seems to have greatly venerated the pope, offered him refuge in his territory, and Matilda's knights accompanied him to the border. Everywhere

Italians poured out to cheer him and beg his blessing. He had the consolation of visiting Monte Cassino for a few days of rest and prayer. Duke Robert brought Gregory to Salerno, the strongest refuge he could offer. He showed him the cathedral of St. Matthew he had had built, and begged the pope to consecrate it, which he did. St. Gregory, however, was nearing his end. He was close to seventy, worn out with labor, and increasingly weak.

Matilda, having returned to Tuscany and won a resounding victory over yet another attack from Henry's forces, hastened to Salerno to visit her spiritual father and found him near death. His last blessing was for her. St. Hugh of Cluny was there too, and from him St. Gregory received the Viaticum. He is reported to have said, shortly before his death, "I have loved justice and hated inequity; therefore I die in exile." To which St. Hugh responded gently, "Nay, Holy Father, in exile thou canst not die, who as Vicar of Christ and His apostles hast received the nations for thine inheritance and the utmost parts of the earth for thy possession." It was May 23, 1085.

An exile he may have been, but he was also a success: Gregory's policies had succeeded in liberating the Church from secular control and had largely destroyed the evils of simony and clerical impurity. The struggle would later need to be renewed as the same old vices reappeared periodically, but subsequent popes would continue the combat. By the reign of Pope Innocent III in the thirteenth century, the papacy was at the height of its independence, influence, and prestige, although the dreary conflict with the German kings persisted until late in that century. It ended, however, with the victory of the sovereign papacy, the foundations of which had been laid by St. Leo and, especially, by St. Gregory.

As for Henry the incorrigible, Gregory's successor Victor III excommunicated him yet again, but the king was still giving trouble

to Victor's successor Urban II (who had to spend a year on an island in the Tiber because Henry and his puppet pope kept him out
of Rome), and Matilda was once again involved in protecting still
another pope. Henry's last years were as full of turmoil as the rest
of his life had been. In 1104 his own son rebelled against him, and
he was imprisoned and forced to abdicate the following year. With
his habitual resilience, he escaped in 1106 and rallied considerable
support, but shortly thereafter he died. His "Pope Clement III"
had predeceased him, ending his non-pontificate in 1100.

A great age begins

That millennial year, then, in which nothing historically significant happened — much less the Last Judgment — may be
taken as the gateway to a glorious period in history. The three
centuries that followed it included the rise of the papacy to the
highest point of its power and prestige, the development of the European nations, the greatest burst of cultural and institutional creativity in Western history, more saints than one can keep track of,
and more material prosperity. Things might have continued so —
there was no discernible reason why not — but by the end of the
1200s, the germ of a new mentality had begun to emerge. It was
hardly noticeable in the beginning, but it was to bring down upon
Christendom terrible chastisements in the form of war, famine,
pestilence, and above all, intractable heresy. That is the story of
the next chapter.

1517 AD

The Protestant Catastrophe

"All the water of the Elba would not provide enough tears to weep over the disasters of the Reform: the ill is without remedy." Strangely enough these are the words not of a Catholic critic of the Reformation but of one of its major players, Luther's friend Melanchthon. Luther himself, shortly before his death, wrote of his distress at the chaos and proliferation of sects that his teachings had unleashed: "I must confess that my doctrines have produced many scandals. I cannot deny it, and often this frightens me, especially when my conscience reminds me that I destroyed the situation in which the Church found itself, all calm and tranquility, under the Papacy."

If even Protestants leaders came to see the Reformation in this light, it is no wonder that Catholics should view it as a true cataclysm. Historian Paul Johnson has called it "one of the great tragedies of human history, and the central tragedy of Christianity." It was a catastrophe and a chastisement for Christendom, a disaster made all the worse because it was the climax of a series of unprecedented scourges that had been unleashed in the course of the previous two hundred years.

Two centuries before Luther posted his famous theses in 1517, the first of the chastisements that were to demolish medieval civilization had already struck: the famine of 1315 to 1322, which caused mass starvation in northern Europe, with some areas experiencing a death rate of ten percent. It was followed in southern France by seven other famines during the same century.

Even worse disasters followed famine. Less than thirty years later, the greatest plague the world had known — the Black Death — was taking millions of lives in gruesome fashion. The Hundred Years' War between England and France had begun, and the papacy was experiencing a series of setbacks that included the Avignon Papacy, the Great Schism, and the heresy of Conciliarism, according to which a Church council was a higher authority than the pope. As if all that were not enough, a new group of Muslim aggressors, the Ottoman Turks, had invaded southeastern Europe in 1354.

Why was God seemingly punishing the Europe of St. Thomas Aquinas and St. Louis, of St. Gregory VII and St. Francis, and of so many other great and holy Catholics? Of course, secular historians would deny that the disasters of the fourteenth, fifteenth, and sixteenth centuries could have been divine punishments. For them, things in history simply happen, without a higher plan or design behind them. Climate changes occur periodically, wars erupt, diseases spread, and the historian's job is to analyze and record these things, not to look for some transcendent meaning in them. Catholic historians, on the other hand, see history as God acting in that world in which he became incarnate. In this he uses human instruments, and it is not always clear in specific circumstances exactly how and where the hand of God is operating. And certainly we cannot always see the hand of God behind every specific global event.

But often connections do suggest themselves; disasters and catastrophes do appear to be fitting divine responses to moral evils.

So while the catastrophic dissolution of medieval civilization, then, is to the secular historian merely an interesting phenomenon, I am strongly inclined to see it as a chastisement — but a chastisement for what, when the previous age seemed so dedicated to the interests of God and His Church?

The coldness

St. Francis of Assisi had already noticed something amiss in his day, the early thirteenth century. Despite the impression we have of the thirteenth century as a fervent and devout period, Francis saw it as more of a new spiritual ice age. "Charity," he said, "has grown cold."

How could that be, in a century when Pope Innocent III had ordered free hospitals for the poor established in every major city, when even kings and duchesses spent time nursing the sick, when new orders had been founded to preach, to teach, to nurse, and to redeem captives?

St. Francis did not, of course, mean by "charity" only the corporal works of mercy — although he was deeply concerned about them — but had in mind first of all that exclusive and tender love for God commanded by what our Lord calls the "first and greatest" commandment. It was love of God that had grown cold. (It is worth noting that Dante, writing at the turn of the fourteenth century, depicted the punishment of the deepest circles of hell as not the traditional fire but ice.)

The Collect for the Feast of the Stigmata of St. Francis on September 17 (Tridentine liturgy) refers to this growing coldness:

O Lord Jesus Christ, Who, when the world was growing cold, didst renew the sacred marks of Thy passion in the flesh of the most blessed Francis, to inflame our hearts with the fire of Thy love, graciously grant that by His merits and prayers we may continually bear the cross and bring forth fruits worthy of penance.

Another sign of this spiritual chill is the fact that the Fourth Lateran Council of 1215 was obliged to require reception of Holy Communion at least once a year under pain of mortal sin. That this central expression of Catholic piety, not to mention inexpressible privilege, should have to be made an obligation rather than naturally be considered a joy shows us again how religious fervor had diminished. Of course, God responds to sin not just with chastisement but with special grace. Hence we find him revealing himself in an extraordinary way to two holy souls of that same century: he gave to Bl. Juliana the mission of promoting in the Church the Feast of Corpus Christi, to revive devotion to the Blessed Sacrament; and to St. Gertrude at the end of the century he revealed his Sacred Heart.

Medieval society goes commercial

The question remains as to what caused this weakening of fervor and the growth of indifference, even in what appears the most Catholic of ages. Some have pointed to heresies that cast doubt on the Real Presence. Most fizzled out without doing much harm, however — although it took major military force to suppress the bizarre sect of the Cathars that flourished in the south of France and in parts of Austria and Italy. The Cathar teaching that all material things were produced by an evil spirit implicitly attacked Catholic worship of the Body of Christ in the Blessed Sacrament. Still, heresy in the thirteenth century was by no means the influential force within Christendom that it would later become; its time was not yet. The medieval heresies, then, seem to be but a minor cause of the growing indifference, as does the corruption that still surfaced here and there among the clergy.

So there must be another element involved in the weakening of faith and love in the High Middle Ages, and the milieu in which St. Francis grew up might give us a clue. His father was a prosperous cloth merchant in a bustling city-state, at a time when business activity was booming all over Europe. In itself, this was no bad thing. Merchant and craft guilds operated on Christian principles, providing social services to their members, regulating quality of work, paying just wages, and charging just prices. Gradually, however, business was becoming more complex and businessmen more individualistic; moneymaking began to preoccupy them far more during the thirteenth century than it had previously.

A French medieval historian has observed that while early medieval people could certainly be greedy, coveting land, prestige, power, and other things, what he saw in the later Middle Ages was something different. It was the growth of avarice: the love of money. As the business culture grew into what is sometimes called proto-capitalism, Catholic hearts were increasingly divided between God and the world. One fifteenth-century merchant headed the pages of his ledger, "In the name of God and profit." As another historian of the late Middle Ages has put it, "They began to keep two sets of books: one for themselves and one for God."

Our Lord put it more bluntly: "You cannot serve God and Mammon." Hence the radical poverty espoused by St. Francis: God had raised up a saint who told Catholics what was wrong, and had inspired him to teach them the remedy. The world of St. Francis did not seem to take it sufficiently to heart, however. The Franciscan Order did grow with extraordinary rapidity, and masses of people turned out to hear the friars preach. Saintly rulers such as

Elizabeth of Hungary and Louis of France joined the Franciscan Third Order. But apparently that was not enough to effect the degree of spiritual conversion for which our Lord was asking.

It is hard to believe that this increased preoccupation with moneymaking had no effect on the spiritual lives of the fourteenth century's increasingly busy city-dwellers. Love of money might not completely crowd out love of God in one's soul, but it easily destroys spiritual fervor, the taste for time-consuming contemplation and devotions, and zeal for works of charity. Even after the famine and the Black Death, report the chroniclers, people were not less avaricious than before, but rather more so. The heresies that sprouted then somehow did more damage and took firmer hold on minds than earlier ones; the heterodox ideas of John Wycliff in England and Jan Hus in Bohemia had a long run in their respective countries. All this, combined with the troubles that plagued the papacy and neutralized its resistance to the evils of the day, had weakened the souls of ordinary Catholics, making them more vulnerable to the influences of the sixteenth-century heresiarchs.

A subversion of thought

As for the intellectuals, many of them had become mesmerized during the fourteenth and fifteenth centuries by the new ideas of William of Ockham, whose philosophy of Nominalism subverted the great scholastic synthesis of faith and reason by destroying its philosophic foundation in Aristotelian realism. For Ockham, the human mind is capable of knowing only individual things, not universal concepts (as the realists held); God could not be known through nature; something could be true for faith and false for reason, and vice versa. These are only a few points from a large and extremely complex body of thought, but they indicate a major shift in mentality — from the Classical and medieval confidence in the use of the mind to a theological and philosophical pessimism.

The loss of confidence in reason's ability to demonstrate the existence of God, and the idea of "two truths" (of faith and of reason) made for theological uncertainty and even futility. Nominalism would go on to be popular in Reformation circles; it might even be what caused Luther to turn against reason altogether: "Reason is the Devil's whore," he wrote. "It must be drowned at baptism."

The later Renaissance, in the late fifteenth and sixteenth centuries, also struck a few blows at the tottering structure of medieval civilization. Individualism, already fueled by the new business culture, became a real cult for writers such as Pico della Mirandola, who glorified Man in a way not previously seen in any culture, including that of the Greeks and Romans. Others exalted the "heroic individual," while Machiavelli, with his infamous "the end justifies the means," championed the immoral ruthlessness that an individual determined to maintain his position and power was entitled to exercise. The ideas of both these men represented the antithesis of medieval thought, which valued community over individualism, humility over pride, and Catholic morality in every sphere.

The coming revolt

These elements did not inevitably cause the disaster known as the Protestant Reformation, but they provided a climate that favored its emergence. Spiritual coldness, preoccupation with worldly affairs, individualism, exposure to various heretical notions, and a widespread corruption of thought that severed the connection between faith and reason: all these left minds confused and souls defenseless before the tidal wave that was about to strike.

Ten Dates Every Catholic Should Know

Already we might note a difference between this analysis and the prevailing conventional wisdom about the Reformation's origins. Here is the myth of the Reformation that we have all heard: the Catholic Church had become worldly and corrupt in the sixteenth century. The clergy were immoral, the monasteries were sinks of iniquity, holy things were bought and sold. The situation was everywhere intolerable, and everyone felt that something had to be done. There was general dissatisfaction with the Catholic Church, and a great yearning for a simpler religion more faithful to the gospel, one that put simple people in direct contact with God. At last a courageous German priest, Martin Luther, outraged by the selling of indulgences, stood up and protested publicly. This was the beginning of a great renewal of Christianity that was both inevitable and historically necessary.

Most Protestants have (naturally) bought this scenario, but even many Catholic historians have subscribed to parts of it, perhaps daunted by the near-universality of the myth in textbooks and academia. The reality of the matter, however, is quite different.

In 1991 Oxford University Press published a survey of the question by Euan Cameron entitled *The European Reformation*. It is an excellent and scholarly overview of the Reformation as a whole, including an exploration of the smaller sects and of the religious practices of ordinary people. But it is especially valuable for dismantling many elements of the Reformation Myth. On the claim that corruption of the clergy ignited a widespread popular outcry for reform, for example, Cameron has this to say:

> Extravagant or dissolute priests had been chastised in sermons for at least 150 years before 1500; St. Bernard of Clairvaux wrote long and hard as early as 1150 against clerical avarice. Pope Alexander VI was easily outdone in vice

and political chicanery by John XII (955-964). If the flaws were ancient, so too were the criticisms. Yet the "reforming" agitators of around 1500 seemed to think that theirs was an age of catastrophic decline after centuries of primeval piety. This myth must be seen as a cliché, and a worn-out one at that.

Such an approach brings a breath of fresh air to Reformation studies. Evils there certainly were and had always been. Ordinary Catholics did not expect perfection of corrupt human nature, and did not leap from indignation at clerical bad apples to the idea that the Church itself needed to be scrapped. Indeed, there is no evidence that most Catholics even wanted it to teach something other than what it had always taught. Many were aware that institutional reforms were badly needed — to ensure that bishops did their jobs and that priests were properly educated, for instance. In fact, the Fifth General Council of the Lateran, held from 1512 to 1517, included in the many items on its agenda the discussion of various reforms. Most of its attention was devoted to urgent political questions, however, and its work was hampered by infighting among some of the participants. Perhaps it was a last chance given to the Church to respond vigorously to the apathy and materialism within its ranks; a little later in that same year, 1517, it was too late — Luther had taken his stand.

When considering the Reformation's origins, it is good to remember, too, that large areas of Europe did not fall prey to its ideas. Where the Reformation did succeed, Cameron observes, its success was tied to the practice of subjecting dogma to public debate; in the place of divinely revealed truth authoritatively taught, people were asked to choose what they wanted to believe. In those areas, moreover, religion immediately became mixed with politics. Historian Carlton Hayes has written, "Protestantism was the religious aspect of nationalism." For Cameron, "The Reformation gave large groups of people across Europe their first lessons in political commitment to a universal ideology. In the sixteenth century, religion became mass politics."

Three "reformers": Luther, Calvin, Henry VIII

I am not going to discuss in detail the theological positions of the founders of the three new religions spawned by the Reformation. Besides the fact that it is pointless to speak of the "theological position" of a man like Henry, a thorough discussion would require too much space here. The main novelties taught by the heresiarchs can be found in numerous Catholic reference works. In any case, my concern is less with the theological intricacies of the heretical movement than with the question of why it succeeded. I will merely point out a few features of the new Protestant teaching that seem to reinforce the weakened spiritual state in which much of Christendom already found itself: diminished in tender devotion to God, our Lady, and the Holy Eucharist, preoccupied with making money, and increasingly individualistic. Even the abuse that caused Luther to go public with his new religious ideas — which he had worked out earlier — was the kind that appealed to its age: the sale of indulgences.

The indulgence issue

This outrage was widely acknowledged as such at the time, and even though it was Pope Leo X (Medici) who ordered it, some Church authorities would not allow it in their dioceses. Leo, who wanted money for the construction of the new St. Peter's, and a German archbishop needing to pay gambling debts, joined forces to have indulgences — reductions of the temporal punishment due to sin, including the sins of those in purgatory — offered in return for money. The oft-cited couplet, "When the coin in the coffer clinks, the soul from purgatory springs" might not be an accurate quotation from the preacher Tetzel, but it sums up what the campaign was all about: wholesale grants of spiritual favors in return for cash.

This kind of huckstering was not new; there is a Pardoner working a similar scam in Chaucer's late-fourteenth-century *Canterbury Tales*. What is more interesting is why it worked now. One cannot imagine indulgence sales being so lucrative without both a flourishing economy and a receptive mentality on the part of the moneyed classes. Certainly the businessman, disinclined to do the work of gaining indulgences for himself through prayer and good works, and short on time to pray for his deceased relatives, could see the indulgence market as a boon. Money he had; time he did not. And of course later, when Father Luther told him there was no such thing as indulgences and he could keep his money, he was happier still.

Luther's ideas fit a more active, individualistic age
We can now examine Luther's ideas in the context of his time. His assertion that "faith alone" is necessary for salvation, for example, suited the era well, doing away with the necessity of those burdensome good works. (Luther did not say that good works should not be done; in fact, he said they *should*; but it is only human to conclude that, if something is not strictly necessary for salvation, it can take a back seat.) Luther also said, "The fulfillment of temporal duties is the only way of pleasing God." This deemphasizing of contemplation and the spiritual life must have contributed to the elimination of monasteries and convents in Germany, and to the emphasizing of secular pursuits, including

business. This suited the industrious burghers of the Holy Roman Empire, and fit in with the spirit of the time. We must also recall that it was within the empire that the most relentless struggle for control of Church lands by kings and local authorities occurred during the Middle Ages. Nothing is less surprising than that their descendants should be delighted to find all that prime real estate, which their ancestors had coveted, falling into their laps.

Similarly, the principle that Scripture alone was the rule of faith, and that every individual could interpret it for himself, appealed to an increasingly individualistic mentality. As a modern author has put it, "the God-given mandate to decide what was true and what was heretical devolved from the Church, where it belonged, to the individual."

Calvin's theology paves the way for business

The French preacher John Calvin agreed with Luther on most points, but he placed more emphasis on the doctrine that would become his calling card: predestination. From all eternity, Calvin thought, God determined to create some souls for heaven and others for hell, and nothing an individual did could change the eternal decree. This was an appalling idea to live with, and early Calvinists often suffered anguish at the thought that perhaps they were damned and could do nothing about it.

The theory was somewhat mitigated, however, by the idea that if you were one of the saved "elect," you would be given some signs from God. Believing in Calvinist teaching was such a sign, as was good behavior; the surest sign, though, because it was the most objective, was that your worldly affairs would prosper. This echoes the way God dealt with the Hebrews in the Old Testament, rewarding them with material prosperity if he was pleased with them.

It is only human nature to say to oneself, "If prosperity is a sign that I am saved, I had better hurry up and become prosperous so I will have the sign." This is perhaps putting it too crudely, but an intriguing connection between Calvinism and the rise of capitalism has been made by a number of sociologists and historians. Certainly the elites of the business world following the Reformation were often Calvinists, and their zeal for work and success was undeniable. Calvinism required a strict code of morality that favored capitalist success: diligence, thrift, hard work, and sobriety were cultivated, while playing cards, spending money on colorful clothes, drinking in taverns, and other forms of dissipation were frowned upon and often punished. Business was seen as a "godly" activity. The work ethic was exalted, both in Europe and later in America, to the point that President Calvin Coolidge could say, "The man who builds a factory builds a church; he who works there worships there." In a way, Calvinism brought medieval materialism full circle: religion and moneymaking had become one.

Henry VIII sends England into schism
Unlike Luther and Calvin, Henry VIII did not intend to start a new theological system; he just wanted a divorce, and the pope would not give it to him. When he made himself the head of the Church in England, thus breaking with Rome, he at first created a schism, not a new church. Yet even before he died, after having gone on to get other divorces and execute two wives, ideologically Protestant associates of his had begun introducing changes into the Catholic liturgy.

During the reign of Henry's successors, the Church of England emerged; a new Protestant sect that mingled some Catholic trappings with various European heretical ideas and a strong association with the crown and patriotic duty. Later Calvinists, always the radicals and militant rebels of the Reformation, became particularly influential in England, to the point that, in the seventeenth century, they were able to mount a revolution and execute the lawful king. This Calvinist influence would affect society and economics in both Britain and the United States, where Puritan malcontents founded the first New England colonies in 1620 and 1630. In secularized form, English Calvinist ideas would help shape the American outlook on political, social, and economic life.

Aftermath and consequences

The results of the Reformation are well known. New religions formed, hostile to Rome and generally submissive to the monarchies in which they emerged. The unity of Christendom was permanently smashed, and large parts of Europe, which it had cost the Church so dearly to win during the Dark Ages, were lost. The saints of the Counter-Reformation would win back some of them and reform the abuses within the institutional Church, but great damage had been done and Western civilization would remain infected with Protestant ideas in many areas. Father Frederick Faber, himself a convert from Anglicanism, analyzed many of the effects of the Protestant mentality on Catholics in nineteenth-century England. "It is hard," he observed, "to live among the icebergs and not be cold."

Elsewhere he pointed to one of the most corrosive results, for Catholics, of living with unbelievers:

Holy Scripture describes life very touchingly as a weary land. . . . So it is in religion. We cannot live among unbelievers and enjoy that bright life of the spirit which belongs to those who dwell in ages and regions of faith. They who, lingering in domestic Edens they are loath to leave, consort much with those who are not children of the Church soon become evidently the worse for it, the moment they live at peace with them and cease trying to convert them. Faith, like holiness, suffers a sort of enervation from such society, and languishes in an uncongenial atmosphere. Hence people get strange views about the easiness of the salvability of heretics, and at last sink to making the kindliness of a doctrine the measure of its truth, and that not kindliness to our dearest Lord or to his one Church, but to those who are not his or hers.[7]

Is there a family left among us that does not include at least one unbeliever, whom everyone agrees, out of "kindliness," not to annoy with awkward religious questions?

From the Catholic civilization of the High Middle Ages to the breaking of the Christian world in the sixteenth century, then, the process looks something like this. Avarice and worldliness first produced indifference to the things of God, and love for our Lord grew cold. When not even the numerous saints whom God raised up in the thirteenth century could touch the hearts of Christians to the extent that God desired, Europe suffered the chastisements of famine, war, and plague. In their aftermath, men grew not better but worse — and the popes themselves were punished with schism and heresy. The next and far worse chastisement was the spread of philosophical and theological error throughout Christendom, by charismatic and militant heresiarchs who preached hatred for the Church as well as false doctrine.

This process continues. Indeed, private judgment has reached its logical conclusion in the self-worship of modern man: from "every man his own pope," during the Reformation, to "every man his own king" in the revolutionary period that followed, it is now "every man his own god." True, the Church of the Counter-Reformation, led by saintly popes, spearheaded by the Council of Trent, and blessed with the aid of numerous extraordinary saints in all walks of life, would reform abuses and do great things. The total number of the legions of souls who were lost to her in Europe was perhaps made up by the conversion of the millions in the New World.

Yet it remains that much that was lost has never been recovered, that the Church in the modern world has been almost permanently on the defensive, and that we have all been affected by the intellectual climate change originally introduced by the Protestant mentality. There is every reason for hope, of course, as there always is, and in the next chapter we will see a great Catholic triumph over another great threat, in that same catastrophic sixteenth century.

1571 AD

The Battle of Lepanto:
Our Lady's Naval Victory

By the end of the sixteenth century, Catholic history was in desperate need of another divine intervention. The Church had begun its counteroffensive against the Protestant revolt, but Christendom remained tragically divided, and many parts of it now seemed permanently lost. Violent domestic uprisings and religious wars had wracked one country after another, leaving Europe vulnerable to attack from without, as her enemies were not slow to realize. If the Holy Roman Empire, for example, became sufficiently occupied with the internal upheavals Lutheranism was producing within it, its attention to affairs beyond its borders would diminish and the weak states of Eastern Europe would be at the mercy of any large invading force.

It was just then that a formidable onslaught, one that had been gathering momentum for centuries, prepared to break upon Europe: the Muslim conquerors of Byzantium had slated the West for incorporation into the Ottoman Empire.

Islam on the march

The confrontation between Europe and Islam had been going on since the seventh century, when the Arabs came boiling up out of Arabia and, in spectacularly swift campaigns, had conquered North Africa, Spain, the Holy Land, and much of the Byzantine Empire. In France they had been stopped by Charles Martel at Tours, while the Spanish resistance in the Asturias Mountains grew into the movement that finally ousted the Muslims from Spain in 1492. However, in the East things had gone the other way. In response to a frantic plea from the Byzantine emperor in 1095 and the rousing call of Pope Urban II, the kingdoms of the West had organized a series of military expeditions — the Crusades — to help Constantinople resist Arab and Seljuk Turk aggression and also to recover the Holy Land. Of these only the First Crusade could be called a success, managing to recover Jerusalem for a time. By the thirteenth century, Muslim conquests had reduced the Byzantine Empire to a fraction of its original territory, although Constantinople itself remained unconquered and seemingly impregnable.

Then came the Ottomans. This Turkic people from the Asian steppes, converts to Islam, began to move into areas formerly held by the Arabs and Seljuk Turks, and developed a well-organized state system and powerful military. In the fourteenth century, Constantinople still eluded them, but in the 1350s they acquired a foothold in Europe by way of the Balkan Peninsula. What then should have been a wake-up call for Europe was muted by the sound of the Hundred Years' War and uprisings following the Black Death. The attention of secular rulers was distracted by domestic problems, while the Church in the fourteen and fifteenth centuries found itself preoccupied with the anomaly of the Avignon papacy, followed by the Great Schism of the West. For decades, there were two and sometimes three claimants to the papal throne, and few of the faithful knew which was the true pope. When that issue was finally settled in the fifteenth century, members of the council that settled it began to say that *they* were the highest power in the Church: thus emerged the headache of Conciliarism.

Meanwhile, the Ottomans, under a series of strong and capable rulers, methodically pursued their goal of building a great empire. They developed a number of administrative innovations, one of which is often called, with some imprecision, the "Janissary system." This ingenious scheme for developing single-minded, fanatically devoted soldiers and civil servants involved the kidnaping of young boys from the lands occupied by the Turks, and taking them to the court of the sultan. There they were made into little Muslims — circumcision and all — but were otherwise well-treated and raised to be completely loyal to their master. They underwent several years of education and stringent physical training, at the end of which most seem to have become part of the elite infantry corps and bodyguard of the sultan known as the Janissaries. Some who showed intellectual aptitude were trained further and used in administration, often at the highest levels of the imperial government. Until much later in the empire's existence, the Janissaries were not allowed to own property or to marry, on the theory that their total dedication to the sultan might thereby be compromised.

Groomed for prestigious positions in the Ottoman army and government, and richly rewarded for their services, for most Janissaries the memories of childhood homes and language faded over the years. We will see one such servant of the sultan, however, who did not forget.

In 1453, the Ottoman Turks succeeded in taking the unconquerable city of Constantinople, and Sultan Mehmed made no secret of his future plans: "The empire of the world must be one, one faith and one kingdom," he said. Even then, Europe seemed too self-absorbed to realize its peril (although it is said that the fall of

Constantinople caused the saintly King Henry VI of England to suffer a mental breakdown and die shortly thereafter). Only Eastern Europe was (only too well) aware of its peril, but its heroes fought alone.

The pope, the general, and the saint

The nepotistic Alfonso Borgia had become Pope Calixtus III in 1455. Whatever his other failings, he saw clearly that the Turks must be resisted: "I, Pope Calixtus, vow to Almighty God and the Holy Trinity, that by war, maledictions, interdicts, excommunications, and all other means in my power I will pursue the Turks, the most cruel foes of the Christian name." Calixtus scraped together what funds he could and called for a crusade. Unfortunately, the rulers of the West were too busy with other things to answer the call; the most the pope could do was outfit a few ships to help in the defense of the Mediterranean islands. It was far from enough. With no major obstacles in their path except for the small and ill-prepared forces of the Balkan principalities, the Turks swept north into the territory ruled by Hungary.

Their major objective: the strongly fortified city of Belgrade, protected by its walls and its strategic position at the junction of two rivers. If Belgrade fell, all of southeastern Europe would be open to the Muslim armies. Defense of the city was crucial to Europe's survival, but it seemed almost impossible to develop any coordinated response to the peril; Hungarian lords were divided on whether to fight or fall back and make a stand someplace else. The feudal magnates were reluctant to commit troops to a common effort, and the king also seemed to be of two minds. He had sense enough, however, to appoint John Hunyadi commander-in-chief of the Hungarian army, and this great warrior must have seemed to the Turks to be everywhere at once. He recaptured fallen fortresses, relieved the sieges of beleaguered towns, and repelled several Turkish attacks; in one instance, the enemy fled in panic at his coming. Then he went to the defense of Belgrade.

According to the historian J. B. Bury, "The siege lasted for three weeks in July 1456, and hardly has a more brilliant feat been achieved in the course of the struggles between Europe and the Ottoman Turks than the relief of Belgrade by John Hunyadi and his Magyar army." The army that Hunyadi managed to piece together was pitifully small and untrained. Pope Calixtus had sent a papal legate to try to rally support for the cause, and issued a bull calling Christendom to prayer, penance, and fasting. When plague struck Rome, he refused to flee; as he told an ambassador, the Turks had lost thousands to the plague, but the sultan did not stop his campaign.

In the end, it was the great Italian preacher St. John Capistrano, traveling around Hungary, who galvanized into action those who heard him speak. St. John himself had been at first discouraged by the response to his impassioned appeals, but one day at Mass he saw in a vision an arrow with the words, "Fear not, John. Go down quickly. In the power of my name and of the Holy Cross thou wilt conquer the Turks." He spoke of this vision in his sermons, and his new confidence was infectious. Numerous volunteers flocked to Hunyadi's standard, and breaking through the blockade of Turkish ships with some of the vessels they had collected, the army entered the city on July 15 to the sound of music.

Still the Muslim threat to Belgrade remained, and the Ottoman cannon continued to damage the walls. When it became clear that the Turks were about to cut the city off completely from all outside contact, St. John slipped out of the city, promising to return with an army that would astonish both Turks and Christians. Meanwhile, as the Turkish forces gathered for an all-out offensive, the defenders were dismayed at the sheer numbers of men and especially of artillery, which Hunyadi said was four times as much as the Turks had ever previously assembled. The great Turkish assault on the walls began in the afternoon of July 21, with devastating effect. St. John returned with his "army" — a sparse, motley crowd of untrained men that Hunyadi deemed unsuitable for fighting. According to some reports, he had begun to think that a truce with the sultan was the only way to save at least some lives in this terrible extremity. The saint disagreed, arguing vehemently and promising victory, and Hunyadi at last yielded to his friend and kept up the fight.

The full story of the siege, of the inspired tactics of the defenders on both land and water, and of the crucial final day is too much to tell in detail here. During the fighting, the tireless Capistrano would stand on a high point of the shore, within sight of both Turks and Christians, waving a banner of the cross and calling out the name of Jesus. Throughout those three weeks, he received and blessed new volunteers as they arrived, and helped to evacuate the sick and wounded from the fortress to upstream villages. He hardly slept or ate, although food was plentiful, for now crusaders were coming from Germany, Poland, Bohemia and elsewhere — thousands of them. They were not professional soldiers, but they venerated St. John so highly that they would follow him anywhere. Priests and religious came with the new contingents, celebrating Mass, chanting their office, and hearing confessions. One soldier is said to have remarked, "We have a holy captain. We must avoid all sin." The battle cry St. John gave them was "Jesus, Jesus, Jesus!"

In the last two days of the great battle, July 21 and 22, hope alternated with despair, as the Turks broke into the city and some defenders fled, fearing all was lost. Their opponents had managed to fill in the moat around the fortress, and before dark on July 21, the Janissaries had swarmed across the moat and up the walls. The tide turned again, however. Hunyadi had the defenders hurl all kinds of flammable material (including slabs of bacon) into the moat and ignite them. The moat became a sheet of fire, separating the Janissaries inside the city from their comrades outside, while those in the moat perished or were badly injured. The defenders then concentrated on the enemy within the walls, and massacred them. By the morning of July 22, it appeared that the battle was won. The remnants of the Turkish army were still large, nevertheless, and the wary defenders were forbidden to pursue them, lest they stumble into an ambush.

Then a strange thing happened. It seems that a handful of crusaders sneaked out of the city to a position opposite the Ottoman lines and began exchanging insults with some of the Turks. Apparently they were viewed as merely a nuisance by a distracted enemy preoccupied with its wounded and the disarray of its forces. Then a small group of crusaders began firing on some regrouping Turks, who fled, and soon a large number of other Christians began to leave cover and attack against orders. St. John went out to the field to call them back, but when defenders inside the fortress saw him, they rushed out to join him. Seeing such a throng approaching, the Turks began to flee and the Christians rushed forward, capturing the Turkish siege guns without a fight.

St. John began to see God's will in this spontaneous advance, and shaking off those who would have restrained him, he followed the crowd and climbed onto a heap of dirt with his standard-bearer next to him. There he cheered the Christians on as they battled the Turkish reserves, waving his cross and shouting prayers. At dusk, they returned to the fortress; the Turks withdrew to their camp, eager to leave the place as soon as possible. They had lost about fifty thousand men, plus three hundred guns and some thirty boats. Belgrade was saved.

Now was the time, thought Hunyadi, to pursue the Turks, to drive them completely out of Europe. He quickly wrote to the pope, arguing that it could be done "if Christendom were to rise." Then only a few days after the battle, he died of illness. St. John did not long survive him. He, too, fell ill, and by the end of October he was dead. Christendom did not rise, and the Turks would return.

A new warrior takes up the fight

John Castriot, the ruler of Epirus — part of modern Albania — had been forced by the Turks to agree to harsh peace terms in 1423. These included the cruel provision of sending his four young sons as hostages to the Ottoman court, where they were apparently circumcised, forced to convert to Islam, and trained to serve the sultan. What happened to three of the brothers is conjecture, although there were rumors of death by poison; they disappear from history. The fourth brother, George, did not. He pleased the court with his military prowess and was soon winning battles for the Ottoman armies. So strong, brave, and skilled was he that the Turks called him *Iskander bey*, their name for Alexander the Great, and he is known to history as Scanderbeg.

The chronology and events of his early career are somewhat uncertain. One version of his story holds that at some point, he secretly returned to Christianity, and when the sultan decided to conquer Albania, in 1443, he escaped from the court and made his way into his native land, where he took charge of its defenses. Another version places him in Albania in the same year, but still leading the Ottoman army against the army of John Hunyadi, who had moved south to meet the Turks. According to this version, at a crucial moment Scanderbeg, along with other Albanians in the Turkish front lines, went over to the Hungarians and fought alongside Hunyadi to win the battle against the Turks.

Both versions are possible; what is certain is that in that year he left the service of the Ottomans and became the Albanian national champion, uniting his country and holding off the Turks until his death in 1468.

Thus it was that after the death of Hunyadi, Pope Callixtus saw Scanderbeg as the last great warrior left to fight for Christendom: "standing almost alone, like a stone wall," he said. He made the Albanian general of the anti-Turkish crusade in 1457, when Scanderbeg was engaged in the grim struggle for the liberation of Albania and the preservation of its freedom from Turkish rule. So successful was he that the sultan acknowledged him as absolute sovereign of Albania in 1461. Pope Callixtus's successors, Pius II and Paul II, continued their desperate calls for a new crusade, but were constantly frustrated by the apathy of Europe. With what scant support the pope and some Italian nobles could give him, Scanderbeg, the "Champion of Christ," continued battling the Turks into his sixties. When he died of a fever in 1467 or early 1468, the sultan is said to have exulted, "At last Europe and Asia are mine. Woe to Christendom! She has lost her sword and her shield!"

How true this was for Albania. A large new Turkish army had been sent against Albania in 1467, which Scanderbeg spent his last months fighting, and when he was gone, his exhausted forces were unable to prevail against it. Albania was almost completely overrun by Turkish armies and thousands were sent into slavery, although a kernel of resistance, as well as the Faith, survived along with Scanderbeg's memory. The Ottomans were now that much closer to becoming neighbors of Western European powers. The

Republic of Venice, in particular, possessed territories on the lower Adriatic coast, for which Christian Albania had served as a buffer, and only the Adriatic itself separated Ottoman Albania from Italy. In the following century, the Ottoman threat to all of Europe would become far graver with the emergence of the empire's greatest sultan: Suleiman.

Suleiman the Magnificent

Suleiman was not only a powerful ruler and a masterful planner of Ottoman campaigns, but also a great patron of the arts. From the buildings he erected to beautify his capital to the beautifully illuminated literary works produced under his patronage, his legacy justifies his sobriquet "the Magnificent." Under his reign, which lasted from 1520 to 1566, the Ottoman Empire was at the height of its power. The Black Sea was a Turkish lake; the Turks controlled the Persian Gulf and all the trade routes to the East. North Africa from Egypt to Algeria belonged to them, while the Moors, defeated at Granada in Spain in 1492, were eager to ally with the Ottomans and reinvade the Iberian Peninsula.

Determined to conquer Europe, which was now not only preoccupied with its petty politics but also divided by the Reformation, Suleiman began his great campaign in the spring of 1521 by capturing the still-crucial city of Belgrade. The following summer he conquered the island of Rhodes, heroically defended by the Knights of St. John. In a chivalrous gesture, the sultan allowed the survivors — knights, soldiers, and civilians — to leave the island alive.

It was then time to prepare for the great move on Hungary, gateway to Europe. Professing to be offended because the young Hungarian King Louis had not congratulated him on his accession, Suleiman assembled an enormous army of some 70,000 regular soldiers and up to 40,000 irregulars, and began to move north. Europe was fully aware of these movements, and had the new Holy Roman Emperor not been so hard-pressed by the Lutheran revolt and its attendant peasant uprisings, he might have been able to take action. (Martin Luther might even have seen the Turkish onslaught as favoring his side, since he advocated pacifism toward the enemy, saying "to fight against the Turks is to resist the Lord, who visits our sins with such rods.") J. B. Bury writes, "The diffusion of the doctrine of the Reformers seems to have been one of the causes which slackened and weakened the resistance of Hungary to the Ottoman invasion."

As the danger drew closer, Luther changed his tune and began to urge princes to support the emperor in a crusade — although he still maintained that the disasters of the Ottoman offensive could somehow be blamed on the popes and bishops. Still, Hungary faced her fate virtually alone. The nineteen-year-old King Louis left his capital to meet an army of close to 100,000 with 3,300 men. By the time he reached the plain of Mohács, where the battle would be fought, his army had increased to perhaps 25,000 — still outnumbered four to one. The result was a forgone conclusion: on August 29, 1526, the Hungarian forces were routed, the king died in the retreat, and most of the country fell under Turkish rule for two centuries.

In 1529 Suleiman turned his attention to his next target, Vienna: the gateway from Eastern to Western Europe. It was in a strong strategic position, not only because of its walls but also because of the protection afforded it by the hilly Viennese woods, impassable for a large army. If Suleiman could only take this city, the Ottoman army could roll west for many miles without encountering serious obstacles. It was late in the season when he began his siege of the city, due to the constant rain that had delayed his approach. The rain had turned to snow by the time he withdrew, after failing to breach the defenses. The sultan tried once more three years later, but again began the siege too late — this time due to the heroic resistance of a Hungarian border fortress that had held up his advance. Once more he was forced to withdraw. Unable to conquer the city, Suleiman vented his rage on the people of the Austrian countryside instead, pillaging and destroying fields and villages.

Suleiman the Magnificent never entered Vienna. Not until the following century would the Turks mount their last and most formidable attack on that city, and then there would be a new generation of heroes to rout them for good.

The sultan's days drew to a close, and in 1566 he finally died during the siege of yet another stubborn and heroic Hungarian fortress, Szigetvár. He left his son, Selim II (known as The Drunkard), an empire of 40,000 square miles, an undefeated fleet, and the dream of being sole emperor of the world. But Selim was not the man his father was. Suleiman could be ruthless and cruel — he had one of his own sons strangled in his presence — but he also had a chivalrous and magnanimous side and he was a highly capable ruler. The weak, inebriated Selim spent most of his reign under the influence of his Grand Vizier, Sokolli, and his reign included atrocities and duplicity that do not seem to have been a feature of the gallant Suleiman's regime. Yet it was during Selim's reign that the Ottomans began their great assault on the Christian Mediterranean. Not only did they soon conquer most of the islands in the eastern part of the sea, but the Moors in North Africa, who had been calling for Ottoman help in reinvading that country since 1567, now thought with good reason that they would soon get it. There were still many Moors left within Spain, and the combination of internal revolt and external attack might be devastating.

The Battle of Lepanto: Our Lady's Naval Victory

Would Europe react *this* time, to such a proximate threat? It was known that the Turkish fleet was on the move, although news traveled slowly; still, if the pope was aware of the general menace, so were the courts to which he sent his diplomats.

Pope St. Pius V sounds the alarm

One man, at least, saw the danger with great clarity; as the menace moved ever westward in 1570, Pope St. Pius contacted the chief rulers of the West to unite against an enemy that threatened them all. In vain. Elizabeth of England? "The cold queen of England is looking in the glass," as Chesterton would write in his famous epic poem "Lepanto," absorbed in herself, her rivalry with Spain, her intricate diplomacy, and her persecution of Catholics. France? "The shadow of the Valois is yawning at the Mass." France at this time was actually a sometime-ally of the Turks, and in the 1570s the country was torn by religious warfare and ruled by the unstable Charles IX, one of a series of sickly sons of the Machiavellian queen mother, Marie de Medici. Even Philip II of Spain, champion of the Catholic cause against the Protestants, was much occupied with his new American empire and did not answer the papal summons in person.

He did, however, send his half-brother, Don Juan of Austria, a young man in his twenties, as well as dozens of ships. Once in Italy, Don Juan was joined by volunteers from all the Mediterranean countries and set about assembling a fleet in 1571. He managed to get about 208 ships (some eighty fewer than in the Turkish fleet), mainly contributed by the Papal States, Spain, and Venice, with a few from other Italian states. The allied states came to be known as the Holy League.

On the flagship of the Genoese admiral, Giovanni Andrea Doria, was a curious picture that Philip II of Spain had sent him.

Philip had received it from the archbishop of Mexico, who had commissioned it as a copy of the mysterious image of Mary that had appeared in 1531 on the cloak of an Aztec Indian. The archbishop, hearing the news from Europe of the Turkish offensives and the scramble to organize an effective defense, must have thought of the many miracles already associated with the image of Our Lady of Guadalupe. When the copy was finished, he touched it to the original and sent it to the king, advising him to display it on one of the ships of the Holy League, in the hope of victory. Pope St. Pius was also seeking our Lady's aid, through the recitation of the Rosary, which he asked all of Europe to pray for a successful outcome of the Christian offensive. When the ships set out from the Sicilian port of Messina on September 16, 1571, all of the men had rosaries too.

Turkish atrocities galvanize the West

There had been much squabbling among the members of the league over organization and tactics; some preferred a more defensive stance, while others were for seeking out the Turks and giving battle quickly. As the fleet moved slowly eastward, it stopped briefly at Corfu. What the men found outraged and horrified them: the Turks had just attacked the island, leaving churches desecrated and religious objects mutilated. Their resolve stiffened, and they resumed their route. Then they came to hear of even worse atrocities that had occurred a few weeks earlier.

In August Ottomans had besieged the island of Cyprus, a Venetian trading colony, and the city of Nicosia had been forced to surrender and accept Turkish peace terms. The Turks, however, immediately broke the agreement, murdering thousands of defenseless citizens. The women fought fiercely to avoid being captured and sold into slavery in Turkish harems; some leaped from the roofs to avoid capture. When several hundred women and boys were captured and put on a ship bound for the slave markets of Turkey, one young woman, Amalda de Rocas, managed in desperation to ignite the gunpowder on board and blow up the ship.

It was then the city of Famagusta's turn. Again, a city driven to surrender trusted to the written promises of the Turkish besiegers that the inhabitants would be spared, and again the enemy refused to honor their own terms. The residents of the city were massacred, while the brave commander, Bragadino, was flayed alive, his skin stuffed, and his corpse dragged through the city. These incidences of Turkish cruelty and treachery galvanized the resolve of the Holy League warriors, especially two of Bragadino's brothers who were ship commanders.

The great battle

In Rome, Pope Pius had been meeting with his treasurer. Suddenly he rose, went to the window, and stood gazing intently at the sky. Then, turning, he said, "This is not a moment for business; make haste to thank God, because our fleet this moment has won a victory over the Turks." The day was October 7, 1571, and what the pope apparently saw in vision — for the news could not possibly have reached him by natural means — was what has since been called the greatest sea battle since the Battle of Actium (between the forces of Mark Antony and Cleopatra, on the one side, and Octavian on the other) in 31 BC.

Naval historians have analyzed it extensively, describing the maneuvering of the two fleets and the various tactics and weaponry used, and several websites provide maps and pictures as well as details. I will not go into the technical questions here, but a few points should be mentioned.

The Turkish fleet was anchored in the Gulf of Corinth as the allied fleet approached. It probably outnumbered the Christian fleet, but the number of combatants seems to have been about equal; perhaps 30,000 on each side. The Christians had the considerable advantage of possessing six galleasses; these were larger than galleys and had side-mounted cannon — as opposed to the front-mounted cannons of the galleys. This allowed them to inflict great damage on any ship that came broadside to them.

Some accounts say that as the fleets came within fighting distance of each other, early in the morning of October 7, the wind favored the Turks and blew their ships forward against the Christian vessels. Then the wind shifted, and Don John's ships were able to draw close to the enemy. This was necessary, because sixteenth-century naval warfare included hand-to-hand fighting on the decks as well as bombardment by cannons and arrows.

Thus the Christian victory at Lepanto would be dearly bought. In Chesterton's graphic words:

> *Don John pounding from the slaughter-painted poop*
> *Purpling all the ocean like a bloody pirate's sloop*
> *Scarlet running over on the silvers and the golds. . . .*

The sea was red with blood for miles around the battle site, when by the late afternoon of October 7, it was all over. The Holy League lost about 8,000 men and at least double that number wounded, but only a dozen ships. Around the same number of Turks died, but thousands more were captured, fifty ships were sunk, and at least 117 vessels were captured.

An unforeseen development was the rising up, from the depths of the Turkish galleys, of several thousand Christian slaves who had been forced to row the ships. Chesterton describes the

> *Thronging of the thousands up that labor under sea,*
> *White for bliss and blind for sun and stunned for liberty.*

The Battle of Lepanto: Our Lady's Naval Victory

Vivat Hispania! Domino Gloria!
Don John of Austria has set his people free.

One famous Spaniard who fought in this battle, the author Cervantes, serves as a symbol in the final verses of the great poem:

Cervantes on his galley sets the sword back in the sheath
(Don John of Austria rides homeward with a wreath.)
And he sees across a weary land a straggling road in Spain,
Up which a lean and foolish knight for ever rides in vain,
And he smiles, but not as Sultans smile, and settles back
    the blade.
(But Don John of Austria rides home from the Crusade.)

When the news reached Europe, there was general relief, rejoicing, and thanksgiving. As for Pope Pius, he gave credit where it was due, declaring October 7 the Feast of Our Lady of Victory; it was later changed to the Feast of Our Lady of the Rosary.

A story without an end

The overwhelming significance of this great battle, the climax of the long Christian resistance to Muslim conquest, was that it ended any major Turkish attacks on the Mediterranean. The decimated Ottoman fleet would be partially rebuilt, and one or two islands and African coastal areas would later fall to Turkish attack, but never again would the Mediterranean be in such serious peril from the Turks as it had been before October 7, 1571. Spain would not be reinvaded by the Moors, and the rest of the southern shores of Christendom would be safe. One of the two main pathways to conquering Europe for Allah had been cut off for good.

True, the Ottoman armies were still intact, and in the following century would mount one last campaign against Vienna. It would be their downfall. From the successful defense of Vienna, Christian armies would go on to roll back Turkish conquests from Hungary and much of the Balkans, although a few areas would not be liberated until the earlier twentieth century. With the help of Mary, as both Our Lady of Victory and Our Lady of Guadalupe, Christian saints and heroes of the sixteenth century had begun that liberation.

By the early twentieth century, the Ottoman Empire was known as "the sick man of Europe," with European powers anxious to dismantle the patient and divvy up his possessions. They got their chance after World War I, when the present states of the Middle East were created as British and French "mandates."

One might have thought at that time that any further threat to the West from Islam was a pipe dream. Instead, it turned out to be a nightmare, one that has now come true. The British agents who taught the Arab subjects of the Ottomans to revolt against them found that — surprise — they later did the same to their Western "saviors." When those saviors then placed a Jewish state in the midst of the volatile nations they had arbitrarily created, they raised Arab consciousness still further. The rest we know. We might yet have need of another Hunyadi, Scanderbeg, or Don John of Austria in our time.

1789 AD

The Age of Revolution

June 17, 1689: "Make known to the eldest son of my Sacred Heart that, as his temporal birth was obtained by devotion to my Holy Infancy, so will he obtain his birth into grace and eternal glory by consecrating himself to my adorable Heart. It wants to triumph over his and, through him, over the hearts of the great ones of the earth. It wants to reign in his palace, be painted on his standards, and engraved on his arms, so that they may be victorious over all his enemies. It wants to bring low these proud and stubborn heads and make him triumphant over all the enemies of holy Church."

These are the words of our Lord to St. Margaret Mary during one of his apparitions to the holy sister of the Visitation Order in Paray-le-Monial, France. The eldest son in question is the great "Sun King," Louis XIV, called "the God-given (*Dieudonné*)" because his birth was the result of the insistent and public prayers of his parents and his people for an heir to the throne. Now God was asking for a return of the favor. He would begin the reign of his Sacred Heart on earth in the palace of Louis, from which it would spread throughout the world. This unprecedented grace offered to the world was to come through the king of France, "the eldest daughter of the Church," the nation of Clovis, Clotilda, Charlemagne, Louis IX, and Joan of Arc. It was refused.

Whether on the advice of his confessor, because of his own pride and vainglory, or for some other reason, Louis did not comply with God's request. One hundred years later to the day, on June 17, 1789, the declaration of a National Assembly and the sovereignty of "the people" by French revolutionaries signaled the imminent fall of the monarchy and the unleashing of a chastisement that has not yet run its course. The Age of Revolution had begun.

The coldness, again

Was the catastrophe that was to consume Europe and sow the seeds of rebellion everywhere merely a punishment for a proud king's refusal of God's requests? It was that, but it seems there were other reasons as well for the chastising of Christendom. In his second revelation to St. Margaret Mary in 1674, our Lord had showed her his Heart and complained to her of the ingratitude of men: "This wounds me," he said, "more than all I suffered in my Passion. All I did for them I count as little and would wish, if possible, to do more. But, in return for my eagerness, they give me nothing but coldness and rebuffs." A year later, during the third revelation, he uttered these famous and solemn words: "Behold this Heart, which has loved men so much, even to suffering and death, to show them its love. And in return I receive for the most part nothing but ingratitude, irreverence, and sacrilege, the coldness and contempt which they show me in this sacrament of love."

The remedy that our Lord had already proposed to St. Gertrude for the coldness of the thirteenth century was devotion to his Sacred Heart. It remained a private devotion, practiced by some religious houses and individual fervent souls in the course of the next centuries. But still the coldness grew. By the seventeenth and eighteenth centuries, Protestantism had penetrated most of

Christendom, casting the chill of ridicule and disdain over traditional devotions and contemplative practices.

Within the Church itself during this period there emerged the heresy of Jansenism, a sort of Catholic Puritanism that included some Calvinist ideas such as a denial of free will and the impossibility of resisting grace, and Quietism, which preached spiritual passivity as the way of perfection. Acts of faith, hope, and charity were unnecessary, according to the Quietists, as was the desire for heaven and fear of hell. Such heterodox ideas contributed to the lack of fervor and tender love for the Sacred Heart of which our Lord complained; indeed, there was even active opposition to the devotion, which Catholics in several countries had begun to practice.

Among the Catholic clergy of the seventeenth and, particularly, the eighteenth century, some bishops were living worldly lives in luxurious style, and clerics of all ranks were among those fascinated by the latest "enlightened" ideas and political schemes. Many, too, were men without vocations who had gone into the Church because it was the destiny of younger sons in their families, or because they had received an ecclesiastical office as a reward from a political or clerical patron. Their worldly distractions might partially explain the spread of a certain "coldness," not only toward God but also toward the destitute and unfortunate during the eighteenth century. A hundred years earlier, St. Vincent de Paul had inspired a great interest in the relief of the poor and the establishment of charitable institutions, but by the eighteenth century, only half as many hospitals and other refuges were being founded. Yet these were more than ever needed as the number of beggars grew alarmingly and the crime rate rose. On the eve of the Revolution, France was still a Catholic country, but her spiritual life and social order were in growing disarray.

Sins of the kings

As for the kings themselves, by the seventeenth century they had long ceased to be models of morality for their people; some of them were in fact among the most notorious libertines of a morally lax age. Louis XIV was not the first French king to flit from mistress to mistress, despite a good and long-suffering wife, but he certainly flouted them in high style. He was also a headache to the Church, with his misguided attempts at making the Church in France more "independent" of Rome. Some have thought that, in his overblown pride, he actually flirted with the idea of making himself the head of the Church in France, as Henry VIII had done in England. But Louis was too much of a Catholic to succumb to that temptation, if he ever entertained it, and he died piously in 1715.

Although the early part of Louis XIV's long reign had been gloriously successful in promoting French political power, domestic prosperity, and culture, things turned sour in his later years. All his wars went wrong, and France was left defeated and in mounting debt. The country was increasingly impoverished and the king widely blamed — it seems justly — for not paying more attention to the social welfare of his people than to his wars. One wonders if he ever connected the abrupt change in his fortunes with the fact that he had not done the one thing that God had — in an unprecedented intervention in history — asked him to do. In the one thing that mattered, the Sun King, for all the glory of his reign, was a failure. His nation and his descendants would suffer for it.

Louis XV (1715-1774) was even more profligate than his father, periodically repenting and sending away the current mistress, only to relapse again into adultery. He also allowed himself to be influenced by these women, particularly when he took France into the disastrous Seven Years' War, despite the absence of any compelling

motive of national interest, at the whim of one Mme. de Pompa-
dour. He may have known about the requests of the Sacred Heart
— members of his own family certainly practiced the devotion —
but he took no steps to implement it.

The Huguenots seek revenge

Of those outside the Catholic Church, the French Calvinists
(known as Huguenots) were particularly hostile to the French
kings because of grievances dating from the previous century. In
an effort to end the civil wars that had wracked France during the
Reformation, the French King Henry IV had issued the Edict of
Nantes in 1598, granting toleration to the Huguenots. In the following century, these industrious followers of Calvin had organized themselves to the point where they kept their own fortified
towns and a private army and navy, and maintained diplomatic relations with England and other Protestant states. Such was their
growing strength that even Cardinal Richelieu, young Louis XIII's
worldly prime minister, who was usually quite willing to support
Protestant states for political reasons, had in the interests of national unity and security launched a successful military campaign
against the Huguenot strongholds and dismantled them.

Thus, by the reign of Louis XIV (1643-1715), the Huguenots
were no longer politically independent, but the Sun King saw them
as a thorn in the side of France. He watched in horror and indignation as English Calvinists organized the Puritan Revolution in the
1640s, which ended in the execution of the lawful king, Charles I,
who was Louis's own uncle, and the dictatorship of the fanatic
Cromwell. For the first time in European history, subjects had
dared to put on trial and execute a "divinely appointed" monarch.
The revolutionary character of Protestantism was thus revealed
more clearly than ever before. As the nineteenth-century French

thinker Auguste Comte would observe, "All revolutionary ideas are only social applications of the principle of private interpretation [of the Bible]." Quoting Scripture (the Old Testament preferred), Calvinist militants were out to transform England into their idea of a "righteous Commonwealth."

Naturally, Louis XIV wanted none of this. He wanted his country to be unified religiously as well as politically, and to that end he encouraged attempts to convert the Protestants, sometimes pressuring them by heavy-handed and sometimes even cruel means. By 1685 he seems to have thought that he had succeeded to the point at which the Edict of Nantes was no longer necessary, and he proposed to revoke it. Pope Innocent XI tried to tell him it wasn't a good idea, but sun kings are bad listeners. Louis revoked the edict, kidding himself that all the Huguenots would become instant Catholics and loyal subjects; instead, some 200,000 of them left the country. They took with them gold and technical skills, and worked with France's enemies abroad, sometimes joining foreign armies against their country. (The descendants of some of them fought for the Germans against the French in World War I.) Those who stayed in France became disaffected, and engaged in sporadic revolts when they got the opportunity.

Louis had converted the Huguenots, all right — into enemies of the monarchy.

The sneers of Voltaire
herald a cultural upheaval

The eighteenth century was termed, by its own trendy intellectuals, "the century of light." This "Enlightenment" refers to a mentality taken up by an international elite, generally atheist or agnostic; it counted Americans such as Franklin and Jefferson among its devotees. The worship of science had become a new craze, and these social and political thinkers believed that all of life should be conformed to the "laws of nature" recently discovered by scientists such as Newton. Spinoza, at the start of the craze for mathematical science in the previous century, had declared, "I shall consider human activities and desires in exactly that same manner as though I were concerned with lines, planes, and solids."

The new social thinkers — known as *philosophes* — among them the witty, malicious, and thoroughly materialist Voltaire, were fired up with the desire to eliminate "unscientific" and "irrational" elements from the new society they hoped to construct. Religion had to go; it was insufficiently scientific. Catholicism in particular was to be destroyed: "Crush the infamous thing," cried Voltaire. Customs, traditions, all the old ideas were out, including the quaint notion of Original Sin, which considered human nature as weak and prone to evil. Nonsense, said the enlightened. Human nature is good and reasonable, if only it be set free from the trammels of custom and religion. This new "liberalism" espoused "freedom from" whatever a thinker found objectionable. For the economically minded, it meant free-market economics with no regulation by the state; for the would-be political leaders of the new world order that existed in their heads, it meant free citizens somehow running their own affairs in a strictly rational way. For nearly all of the most daring and advanced thinkers, it meant destruction of Christian morality, the Catholic Church, and the monarchy.

For a *philosophe* like Jean-Jacques Rousseau, a back-to-nature man, freedom meant liberation from all the constraints of civilized life. Rousseau would write one of the seminal works in progressive education: *Emile*. This treatise recounts the "education" — if it can be called that — of an imaginary child left perfectly free to "learn by doing."

"When I get rid of children's lessons," wrote Rousseau, "I get rid of the chief cause of their sorrows; namely, their books. Reading is the curse of childhood." Generations of progressive educationalists have since eaten this stuff up, without bothering about Rousseau's qualifications for writing it.

Rousseau had but one teaching job in his life, as a private tutor, but he became so angry with the children that he quit, afraid that he might harm them. True, he had five children by his mistress. No sooner was each born, however, than he deposited the baby in the nearest orphanage, where it is assumed the child did not long survive. So much for hands-on experience. So where did Rousseau get his ideas? Like all the other Enlightenment folk, he made them up; they are abstractions, with almost no basis in reality. They are, indeed, recipes for creating a new reality — exactly what the French revolutionary heirs of the Enlightenment would claim to do.

The ideas of this gang were spread through the press, which was remarkably and excessively free in eighteenth-century France. Courtiers in the king's palace laughed at the latest barbs of Voltaire, and noble lords and ladies applauded subversive plays, with no thought of where these daring notions might lead. It seems that among the French lower classes, at least in the cities, literacy was common and so was reading; pamphlets and novels designed to give this class a sense of its grievances proliferated. For radicals like Voltaire, relentless ridicule of the people, classes, and ideas of which they disapproved was the weapon of choice, and readers eagerly devoured it.

The gracious meetings of the cultural elite at the homes of hostesses with money and social skills, known as the *salons*, were another way of diffusing ideas. Favorite guests often included interesting foreigners such as Benjamin Franklin, making for an international flow of ideas. The secret lodges of Freemasonry, founded in England in 1717 and rapidly spread to the continent and to England's colonies, were a major channel for Enlightenment thinking. Even some of the Catholic clergy were Lodge members during this period. Like the rest of those whose doom had been decreed by the very people they found so entertaining, the clergy, too, were incredibly slow to realize the total incompatibility of the new ideas with the Faith.

It is an interesting phenomenon that the most militantly "rational" and secular intellectual movements appear to stimulate the emergence of what would seem their very opposite. Thus, the Enlightenment period also saw the proliferation of groups dabbling in the occult, hypnotism, and neo-pagan practices. There was a new interest in Gnosticism and reincarnation. The odd thing is that the same intellectuals who preached "rationality" most vociferously were often members of these groups too (such as Freud and Marx in the nineteenth century.) Thus, the enemies of Church and king had more than one means of bewitching the minds of Frenchmen

Of course, there was a Catholic counterattack against all these evils, although some apologists admitted their frustration at trying to counter the malicious satire and sarcasm of men like Voltaire. The great intellectual order of the Church, the Jesuits, should have been on the scene, but under pressure from the Bourbon families of Spain, France, and some Italian territories, Pope Clement XIV agreed to suppress the order on June 8, 1773. "In twenty years," Voltaire then exulted, "nothing will be left of the Church."

The story of how the order's many enemies achieved this victory is too complex to discuss here, but it is worth mentioning that the Society of Jesus had been given the mission by God, through

St. Margaret Mary, to promulgate the devotion to the Sacred Heart. Some — such as St. Margaret's confessor and friend, St. Claude de la Colombière — certainly did so, but too many others did not. The confessors of Louis XIV who seem to have done nothing to influence the king to comply with our Lord's wishes, and might have actively discouraged him from doing so, were — alas — Jesuits. Might not the suppression of the order be seen as a chastisement on them?

The radical duke

In his palace — the Palais Royale in the center of Paris, on the right bank near the Seine — Philippe, duke of Orléans, was delighted with the intellectual and political ferment all around him. He was King Louis XVI's cousin and had often thought how much better equipped for the throne he was than his mild-mannered, ineffective relative. Philippe liked to feel he was part of the avant-garde; he opened his palace to all the most advanced thinkers and most daring politicians, and supported them with his enormous wealth. His vast web of contacts would enable him to play a role in the revolution that is still somewhat obscure, because much of it was secret. He was right at home with the indecent speech fashionable in some circles; at least once he sang lewd songs on the stage, no doubt to great applause. (He would not have done it otherwise.)

We will meet him again in this tale.

As the revolution drew nearer, salons became political clubs, such as the Jacobin Club, the most radical, which originated in Versailles. Others sprang up all over Paris, gathering not merely abstract thinkers but men with practical agendas, busily organizing their factions and ready to act when the time came. In early 1789, the time had almost come.

Louis the would-be loved

Louis XVI and his wife, Marie-Antoinette, daughter of the great Catholic Empress Maria-Teresa of Austria, were young when they unexpectedly inherited the rule of France. They had been married in 1770, when he was sixteen and she fifteen, and four years later, following the unexpected death of Louis's father, they found themselves king and queen. They were so overwhelmed at the responsibility that they knelt down and wept at the news, praying for strength to bear the heavy burden for which they felt ill-prepared.

Louis took his new responsibilities seriously, trying to choose competent ministers, untangle intricate questions of finance, and address the need for reforms in many areas of French politics and society. Many such reforms were enacted; child labor, for example, was prohibited in eighteenth-century France, but only much later in Great Britain and the United States. Louis was so zealous in his reforming projects that too much reform too fast became an unsettling factor in French political life. Often he was so eager to get on to the next reform that he failed to see the previous one through to a successful conclusion.

Above all, he wanted to be loved by his people, and this would prove to be his fatal flaw. Time after time in the course of the early Revolution, he refused to order troops to fire on a mob when such an order could well have turned a still-uncertain crisis in his favor. Still, he was trying hard; he was also devout, honorable, and a good father to his four children. His wife, Marie-Antoinette, after a somewhat frivolous and extravagant period early in her marriage, had settled down to earnest motherhood. Nonetheless her profligate early years made for gossip-mongering, and as a foreigner, she was seen as an easy target for enemies of the monarchy, so attacks on her were relentless. There was an infamous, trumped-up story linking the queen with the underhanded acquisition of a diamond necklace, which was totally false but made a good propaganda tool, and other malicious (and untrue) stories told about her.

The king and queen had their private griefs as well as their public duties and cares: their youngest child, a daughter born in 1786, died within a year; a son born in 1781 died at the age of eight. Their remaining children were Marie-Thérèse, born in 1778, and the dauphin, Louis-Charles, born in 1785. Of these two only Marie-Thérèse would survive the Revolution.

Although King Louis was devoted to God and his people, zealous for reform, and anxious to please, there was one "reform" to which he gave no attention until it was far too late: he did not comply with the requests of the Sacred Heart made to his ancestor, Louis XIV, although his sister Elizabeth had urged him in 1788 to do so. She even wrote out a form of consecration that he might have used.

Prologue: the characters of the tragedy assemble

By 1789 the actors were all in place: the political clubs were organizing demonstrations and reiterating their grievances against the government and their desire for radical change. Duke Philippe was meeting with his cousin's enemies in his palace and helping to finance their political activities. Members of the Grand Orient Lodge of the Freemasons were drawing up plans for a new, utopian France. Radical orators were practicing speeches in their Left Bank café, the Procope. The presses, working overtime, were churning out inflammatory pamphlets and newspapers. It needed only a match to set all this combustible material alight.

Meanwhile, the king had called a meeting of the Estates General for May of 1789. This was a group of representatives from the three traditional divisions of French society: the clergy, the nobility, and the other classes — the "third estate." It was not intended to help govern, as the British Parliament, but to advise; therefore each "estate" had but one vote on the matters that came before it. This ancient political body had not met for over a century, for good reason: the system was outdated by the eighteenth century. The nobility, often short of money, had been increasingly active in business and were intermarrying with the middle classes. The wealthier middle class, and even well-off peasants, were eager to purchase — or attain by marriage — titles of nobility that added to their prestige. And members of the clergy came from all classes. Thus the "estates" were in reality no longer neatly delineated.

Besides calling the meeting, the king had requested feedback from all the provinces on what the concerns of the country really were. These reports (*cahiers*) were largely drawn up by lawyers and political activists; still, while most were concerned with equalizing the tax burden (the king's own priority), none referred to the replacement of monarchy with another form of government.

The atmosphere in the months preceding the historic meeting at Versailles was made more tense by the extreme weather that had begun in the summer of 1788, with devastating hailstorms followed by drought. Then came the harsh winter of 1788-1789. The cold was fierce, and in Paris people were starving. Food distribution was set up in the streets, and the king and queen served up soup to the hungry. As Christmas drew near, Marie-Antoinette took her children into a room in the palace and showed them the toys that merchants had brought her, from which she was to choose the children's Christmas presents. She informed them that all the toys were being sent back and the money used to feed the poor instead; there were children who had no food, let alone toys, and they came first. (So much for the false report that she said, when told the people were clamoring for bread, "Let them eat cake." This infamous statement comes from a work by Rousseau (*Confessions*) in which an anonymous "princess" is said to have uttered it at least two years before Marie-Antoinette arrived in France.)

Following that terrible winter, the spring crops were poor, thus both prolonging the food shortages and increasing general dissatisfaction. And on the fifth of May, the curtain rose on the first act of the French Revolution.

The explosion

Here is the myth of the French Revolution, the one that held sway in modern historiography until quite recently: the French lower classes, especially the peasants, had been brutalized for centuries by the self-serving Catholic clergy and indolent nobility. The kings had been totally indifferent to the plight of the people and had done nothing to reform French society. Finally, driven to desperation, "the people" rose up and overthrew their oppressors, setting up an enlightened republican form of government. This government did very fine things until, some years later, it unaccountably fell under the control of radicals and there was a brief period of terror. On the whole, however, the French Revolution was one of the Good Things of history.

The reality is quite different. I've already mentioned the pursuit of reform by the king and his government (often obstructed by the hidebound traditionalism of those very "people" said to be clamoring for reform.) Furthermore, as a writer on American history has observed, revolutions are never made by "the many." They are made by some of "the few," who mobilize the masses against another group of the few. The real creators of revolution are a revolutionary elite who use the masses to pursue their own agendas. As for the idea that the French Revolution turned nasty only some years down the road, writings from the time show clearly that the goal of eliminating "the privileged" existed from the start.

The full course of the Revolution cannot be adequately presented here, but we can examine a few key events from an unusual perspective: the eyes of a child. The king's son Louis-Charles was four years old when the family went to Versailles, where his father was attempting to satisfy the demands of the estates. It was while the meetings were going on that his elder brother, the *dauphin* or crown prince, became gravely ill with what seems to have been a skeletal form of tuberculosis. The child was sent some distance away to a country place where it was thought the air was better for him. Every day the king met with the representatives of the estates, whose words were daily becoming more heated and unruly, and then made the trip to visit his son. Even after the boy died on June 4, the king's presence was constantly demanded by the assembled delegates. "They do not leave me time to grieve," the father complained.

The third estate demanded a head-count vote, rather than the one vote each estate traditionally had held, and was able to enforce its will when some of the radicalized clergy and nobility joined it. On June 17 it constituted itself as a National Assembly, and the king acknowledged the "sovereignty of the people." (One hundred years earlier, Jesus had asked for his Sacred Heart to reign in France; now he would be replaced by other gods.) Jubilant crowds outside the Versailles house where the royal family was staying shouted slogans, some of them directed against the queen and in favor of the duke of Orléans. However, when Louis-Charles, now the *dauphin*, appeared with his mother and sister on the balcony of the house, the crowds were charmed; but that sentiment would change very soon.

The Assembly moved to Paris, nineteen miles away, to write a constitution, and the king was obliged to attend some of the sessions. The queen was wracked with anxiety for his safety while he was gone, although her son tried to console her: "He will come back, Mama, you'll see. My father will come back!" He did — that time. But soon after the Bastille in Paris was attacked on July 14, a mob marched on Versailles, broke into the palace, and "escorted" the royal family to Paris. Louis-Charles looked out of the carriage and saw the heads of guards he had loved being waved on pikes by the crowd. In Paris, the family lived for a time in the Tuileries Palace, where the children's parents tried to maintain as normal a life as possible. Louis-Charles had other boys to play with, and he was given a uniform with a little sword in which he reviewed his troops. Passersby often conversed with him through the fence. "If I lived here," one woman said, "I'd be as happy as a queen." "Happy as a queen?" the little boy replied. "But I know one who cries every day."

The boy was growing in charity as well as knowledge, anxious to do little things for his mother and to give to the poor what he was able. The measures passed by "the people's" government became more and more oppressive; in the Civil Constitution of the Clergy of July 1790, the clergy were made government employees and required to swear an oath to the Republic. Those who refused — some 90 percent — became enemies of the state, to be tracked down by dogs and executed. The king cooperated with the new government, in a weak attempt to save the situation, but even when he had the opportunity of ordering his still-loyal troops to support an offensive against the revolutionaries — which his wife and friends begged him to do — he refused. He would not shed a drop of "the people's" blood, oblivious of the death toll of ordinary people that was already steadily mounting. Finally, in early 1792, when the demon of the Terror, Robespierre, began to gain power, the palace was besieged by a Jacobin mob, and the family was forced to flee to the Assembly for safety. They were then imprisoned, together with the king's saintly sister, twenty-eight-year-old Elizabeth, who joined them voluntarily.

A family's agony:
prison, torture, and death

Outside the prison walls, the nation was at war with neighboring countries that had become alarmed at the chaos within France and fearful for the safety of the royal family. The emperor of Austria, Joseph II, was the brother of Marie-Antoinette, and other rulers were related to the royal family by ties of blood or marriage. Furthermore, the sacred character of Christian monarchy made the deposition, let alone execution, of a legitimate ruler seem almost sacrilegious. Lastly, there was fear throughout Europe that the virus of revolution would spread beyond France. Within France, economic hardships increased and revolts had broken out against the revolutionary regime throughout the country, especially in the western provinces.

In the Vendée, in western France, there began a large-scale uprising of peasants loyal to their king and to their Church. Because it was the nobility who had military training, the peasants recruited the local landlords (who sometimes needed strong persuasion) to lead them. One of these leaders was François Athanase de la Charette, and an address he made to his motley troops sums up the real issue between the atheist utopianism of the revolution and the mind of Catholic France: "For us, our country is our villages, our altars, our graves, all that our fathers loved before us," he said. "Our country is our Faith, our land, our king. But what is their country? Do you understand it? . . . They have it in their brains; we have it under our feet." How neatly put is this distinction between philosophical idealism and realism!

The persecution of the Church continued, while the new "religion of reason" staged blasphemous farces, such as installing an opera singer dressed as the Goddess of Liberty on a stage-scenery mountain set up in the nave of Notre Dame Cathedral. The loss in art treasures and relics of the saints was incalculable, and the guillotine was rarely silent.

Within Paris's Temple Prison — once a castle for the Knights Templar — Louis attempted to create a semblance of normality for his family. He gave regular lessons to the children, led family prayers, and urged them to get what exercise they could. Above all, he insisted on forgiveness of their enemies. The government was still divided on what to do with him. Tom Paine, the revolutionary pamphleteer, suggested exile in the new United States, but that did not suit the radical Jacobins who were increasingly in control; they wanted Louis dead. Several votes were taken on the question in the National Convention, and in one of them the deciding vote for execution was cast by Philippe of Orléans (now a deputy calling himself "Philippe Equality"). Louis XVI wrote his testament, consecrated his country to the Sacred Heart — too late — and went bravely to his death on January 21, 1793. His seven-year-old son was now Louis XVII.

The violence continued to escalate all that year and into the next, reaching its demonic climax in Robespierre's "Republic of Virtue." "The driving force of . . . popular government during a revolution is both *virtue and terror,*" he proclaimed, and the increasing numbers of the doomed began to include his former associates who were not "virtuous" enough. On his orders, or at least with his knowledge, Louis-Charles was separated from his mother, his sister, and his aunt. In a sickening case of child abuse, he was treated with alternating brutality and indulgence in order to break his will. Depraved guards made him drunk and then taught him words and phrases that he had to repeat. It is likely that he was also maltreated sexually. When, in times of sobriety, he refused to co-operate, he was cruelly punished.

The story his jailors wanted him to tell was that he had been sexually abused by his mother and his aunt, so that this "testi-mony" could be used against his mother at her trial. The govern-ment representatives duly appeared in the boy's cell, took down what his jailors prompted the drunken child to repeat, and had him sign it. That done, there was no more use for him and he was left alone, already suffering from the malady that had killed his brother, and beginning to realize at least some of what had been happening to him. Yet he remained mindful of his father's teach-ing: once, after the jailors had been tormenting him, one of them asked, "What would you do if you were the king and free?" The child replied, "I would forgive you."

At Marie-Antoinette's trial, when her son's supposed deposition was read out, she not only refused to accept it, but she appealed dramatically to the audience: "[N]ature recoils from such an accu-sation against a mother," she cried. "I appeal to all those who may be here!" This elicited such sympathy for her that the session had to be suspended for a time. It went on, of course, with other charges brought, and the queen followed her husband to the guil-lotine on October 16. Her son never knew it; until his own death, he thought she was still in the room just above his own.

Louis was now so neglected that his cell became filthy and his bed linen was never changed. His nails grew but there was no one to cut them; he also grew, but since his clothes were not changed, they became a torture for him — particularly as his health contin-ued to decline. He tried not to speak now to his series of brutal jailors; he was older, and understood more clearly his situation. In May of 1794 his aunt was executed, leaving his sister, Marie-Thérèse, utterly alone. Distraught with grief and fear, she still remembered her father's teaching, compulsively scrawling on the walls of her cell, "I forgive them."

On the outside, things were changing. The revolution had devoured its own to such a point that Robespierre himself had perished. It is satisfying to record that Philippe Equality had already gone to the scaffold on November 7, 1793. He was, after all, an aristocrat and therefore an enemy of "the people" — although he had tried to save his head by insisting that he was not really the son of his father, the former duke, but of a coachman. It did not go over well, and his head rolled. The new government (before it was taken over by Napoleon, an episode that does not concern us here) then considered the question of the royal children. Meanwhile, Marie-Thérèse became part of a prisoner exchange that delivered her to her mother's family in Austria.

Louis-Charles, a few months away from death, was finally given a kind jailor. The guard called him "Your Majesty," and described how he had seen him in the Tuileries gardens in his uniform. Then the child spoke: "Did you see me with my sword?" he asked. He was now given medical care, although it was ineffective, and made as comfortable as possible. On June 8, 1795, he was near the end. In response to a question, he replied, "I'm still suffering, but much less now; the music is so beautiful!" Asked where the music was coming from, he said to the guard, "From above. . . . Don't you hear it?" The man kneeling at his side pretended to listen, although he heard nothing. "In the midst of all those voices," continued the child, "I recognize my mother's!" Later he asked if his sister could hear the music too; "that would do her so much good!" He leaned toward his kind friend and said, "I have something to tell you. . . . " and died. He was ten years old; the last king of France.

His body was thrown into a common grave, to prevent any veneration of his remains. Unknown to the government officials, however, the doctor who performed the autopsy had kept the boy's heart. He took it away secretly and preserved it in alcohol. It survived many vicissitudes and ended up with a Catholic family outside France. Toward the end of the last century, it surfaced again in Paris, and was given DNA testing that proved it to be the heart of Louis XVII. Then, in June of 2004, with great solemnity and accompanied by thousands of devout French legitimists, it was laid to rest in the royal crypt of the Basilica of St. Denis in Paris.

The seeds of revolution spread

Despite the regime of Napoleon and the reigns of a few more "constitutional" kings, several more revolutions in France occurred in the nineteenth and twentieth centuries. "Revolution" came to be seen as a good and liberating process, to be exported to all corners of the world. The heady ideas of the revolutionaries, with their glorification of "the people" and their rights, migrated all over Europe with Napoleon's armies and the new regimes he set up in the countries he conquered. They were carried back to their own countries by soldiers who had fought against France. Polish and Russian officers, for example, formed secret societies devoted to the adaptation of French revolutionary principles to their own nations, and later orchestrated their own uprisings. Virtually every country in Europe had a revolution in the course of the nineteenth century, although the greatest of them all was reserved for the twentieth, as we will see in the following chapter.

Indeed, the heady ideas of the French Revolution continue to influence the world today. The principles that "the people" are

Ten Dates Every Catholic Should Know

sovereign in all things, that hierarchy of any kind is bad, that democracy is the only possible form of government, that women should rebel against the authority of men, laity against clergy, and children against parents, can all be traced to the French Revolution. The false ideologies and self-worship of the *philosophes* are with us still, legitimizing all manner of errors and perversions — and inventing new ones and calling them "rights of man."

With the tyranny and bloodshed that would descend upon Europe in the twentieth century, it might seem as if God had abandoned his faithless people to the just consequences of their actions and ideas. But no — he makes one more attempt to reach them. This we will see in the final chapter.

1917 AD

Fatima and the Twentieth Century

"Make it known to my ministers that, given that they follow the example of the king of France in delaying the execution of my request, they will follow him into misfortune."

These are the words of our Lord to Sister Lucia of Fatima in the summer of 1931. He returned to the subject in August of the same year: "They did not want to heed my request. Like the king of France, they will repent and do so, but it will be late."

A divine last resort

To what do these extraordinary messages refer, with their explicit mention of the failure of Louis XIV to consecrate himself and his country to the Sacred Heart of Jesus? They must be considered within the context of the whole revelation of Fatima, itself intimately connected with the history of the twentieth century, in which the traditional four horsemen of the Apocalypse — war, famine, pestilence, and death — seemed to strike the earth with a vengeance.

It was as if God, stung — to put it in human terms — by the disobedience to his repeated requests, had decided as a last resort to send his mother on a mission to touch the hearts of an increasingly cold and sinful world. Beginning in the mid-nineteenth century, the "Age of Mary" saw an unusual number of appearances of the Blessed Mother, beginning in 1830 with her visit to St. Catherine Labouré in Paris, and continuing with the apparitions of La Salette, Lourdes, and Pontmain. Each time her message was one of prayer and penance for sin.

On September 16, 1838, Bl. William Chaminade, founder of the Marianists, wrote prophetically to the pope of what he saw as the beginning of a new era in history. This age of Mary, he said, would lead to a great triumph for Christ and his Church. In another letter written the following year, he wrote, "To her, therefore, is reserved a great victory in our day, for to her belongs the glory of saving the Faith from the destruction with which it is threatened."

The threshold of disaster

The triumph of good in any form, however, seemed increasingly remote as the twentieth century opened. During the last years of the nineteenth century, optimists — and materialists, who were often the same people — had pointed to new discoveries as heralding an age of progress and peace. During the 1890s, the bacilli that caused malaria and plague had been discovered, as had x-rays; the motion-picture camera and the airship had been invented, and marvels such as the Paris metro and the hydroelectric plant at Niagara Falls had been constructed. What might science not achieve, what might mankind not write upon the blank page of history that was opened on January 1, 1900?

Pope Leo XIII, who in 1879 had begun a reign that would last until 1903, did not take such a rosy view of the world's progress. On October 13, 1884, the pontiff had collapsed after saying Mass — seemingly from a stroke or a seizure — and was rendered briefly unconscious. In fact, it was not a physical problem but a spiritual visitation: Leo had a vision of Satan asking God for more time in which to unleash his power upon the world and the Church, and of God granting him a period of about a hundred years. Following this vision, Pope Leo composed two prayers to St. Michael: a shorter one to be recited after every low Mass, and a longer form of exorcism. He is said to have understood that this period of Satan's formidable onslaught would be followed by the victory of St. Michael and the Church.

Thus, when the year 1900 began, Pope Leo had no illusions about the new century — especially with the heresy of Modernism ("the compendium of all heresies," as St. Pius X was to call it) in full swing. Father Alfred Loisy, one of its leading exponents, was at work on the books that would spread Modernism's false ideas in the seminaries, Catholic schools, and the minds of Catholics. Modernism can be called the application of Darwinism to religion. Everything we thought we believed was really only provisional, because dogma "evolves" constantly. Each new generation, said the Modernist, must discover and create its own theological notions, because solemnly defined doctrines are silly and out of date. It is not difficult to see how such thinking could destroy the Faith in countless souls. We are not free of it yet.

The year 1900 and the horseman of death

Let us look at some of the other developments that occurred in 1900. King Umberto I of Italy was assassinated, in one of the numerous terrorist murders of the period. Anarchists, who aimed at the destruction of all existing public order and social structures, were only one of several groups engaged in terrorism, but between 1894 and 1914, they managed to kill six heads of state. Besides King Umberto, their victims included a president of France, two Spanish prime ministers, the Empress Elizabeth of Austria, and

Ten Dates Every Catholic Should Know

President McKinley of the United States. In 1900 the bloody Boer War was going on between Great Britain and the Dutch settlers of South Africa, and the Boxer Rebellion had erupted in China. This uprising by a pagan secret society was ostensibly directed against the power of foreign interests in China, but it is revealing that while hundreds of foreigners died, thousands of Chinese Christians were killed. In that year, too, Frederick Nietzsche, the anti-Christian writer who despised the weak and exalted the ruthless "Superman," died in an insane asylum; in the coming decades, his works would feed — or rather, poison — countless receptive German minds. In 1900 Sigmund Freud published *The Interpretation of Dreams*, ushering in the era of psychoanalysis, with its irrationality, its obsession with sex, and its materialist outlook.

These news items from the year 1900 foreshadow the bad news waiting in the wings of the new century: terrorist movements, anarchist, Nazi, and Communist, that would set the world ablaze; violent conflict between Western and Asian powers; atheist ideologies disguised as politics or science. Within four years, war had broken out between Japan and Russia, and the resulting economic disruptions caused agrarian unrest and rebellion in Russia, along with thousands of terrorist murders. Between 1905 and 1914, a series of international crises and local wars would bring the world to the edge of the abyss.

Pope St. Pius X, who succeeded Leo in 1903, was no more optimistic than his predecessor had been. In his first encyclical, *E supreme apostolatus cathedra*, he referred to his "terror" at the appalling condition of mankind, because of its abandonment of and apostasy from God. He characterized it as "this monstrous and detestable iniquity proper to the times we are living in, and through which man substitutes himself for God." He wondered, too, "whether such a perversion of minds is not the sign announcing, and the beginning of, the last times, and that the Son of Perdition spoken of by the Apostle [2 Thess. 2:3] might already be living on this earth."

Fatima

The Age of Mary was rapidly becoming the Century of Total War, but she was preparing to enter the fray: to do battle with Satan in the most spectacular series of heavenly visitations in history. As Sister Lucia would tell Father Augustine Fuentes in a conversation in 1957: "In the plans of Divine Providence, God always, before he is about to chastise the world, exhausts all the other remedies. Now, when he sees that the world has not heeded any of them, then, as we say in our imperfect manner of speaking, he offers us with a certain trepidation the last means of salvation, his most holy Mother."

The terrible chastisements of the twentieth century were thus accompanied by the coming of our Lady to a small town in central Portugal. The nature of the Fatima messages, their connection to global events, and the spectacular and public miracle by which they were validated, would be unprecedented in the history of Marian apparitions.

In 1916, three young Portuguese shepherd children, Lucia, Jacinta, and Francisco, were visited a number of times by an angel. Referring to himself as the Angel of Peace and the Angel of Portugal (St. Michael), he taught the children prayers of reparation and urged them to make sacrifices for the conversion of sinners; he particularly mentioned the "outrages, sacrileges, and indifferences" by which our Lord is offended, and referred to the Holy Eucharist as "horribly outraged by ungrateful men."

Then on May 13, 1917, Mary appeared to the children, promising to return on the thirteenth of the next five months.

Ten Dates Every Catholic Should Know

The horseman of war and the great revolution

In that same year, two momentous events were taking place in Europe, although the children could have heard of only one of them. Portugal was fighting in the great world war that had been raging since 1914, when complex diplomatic brinkmanship had resulted in the German invasion of Belgium and France, and set the European continent on fire in a horrifying disaster of death and destruction. Not only did modern military technology make this conflict far more devastating than anything in history up to that time, but its effects were felt far beyond Europe, as more and more nations were drawn into the maelstrom. There seemed no end to the killing in sight, and everywhere there was anxiety and grief for the men at war.

Something else was occurring in May of 1917. Few had probably paid much attention to the disturbances in Russia, beginning in February with food shortages. That nation had in fact been in a precarious condition for several years. Radical groups, including the recently organized Marxists, had been attempting to destabilize the government for decades; between 1906 and 1911, some four thousand terrorist murders had cut down competent men such as Prime Minister Piotr Stolypin, who had implemented a brilliant series of measures in favor of the peasants that greatly increased the prosperity of the country. Worse, the royal family had come under the spell of one of the most bizarre and sinister characters in history, the monk Grigori Rasputin.

Rasputin's shadowy past was reputed to have included participation in secret occult rites, and he was denounced by the local bishop in his native Siberia. Certainly he possessed unusual healing powers. He also accurately foretold Stolypin's murder, pointing to the prime minister's carriage as it passed in the street on September 13, 1911, and crying, "Death is after him!" The following day

Stolypin was assassinated. His reputation for promiscuity earned him the nickname "the Dissolute," and despite his scruffy appearance, Rasputin's St. Petersburg apartment became a magnet for the ladies of the court, over whom he seemed to cast a sort of hypnotic attraction. One of his female followers used to address him as "God," and he did not object.

He entered history when he befriended Czar Nicholas II and Czarina Alexandra, becoming a fixture at the royal palace. The royal couple valued Rasputin for his strange ability to stop the dangerous hemorrhaging of the little crown prince, who suffered from hemophilia. When the child was in torment and doctors could do nothing for the painful internal bleeding, Rasputin would stand at the foot of the boy's bed and look at him. Invariably, it seemed, recovery followed. Once, when the family was on vacation far from home, a particularly violent attack put the prince's life in grave danger. Alexandra telegraphed to Rasputin in St. Petersburg, begging his advice. He replied that she should do nothing, because the child was going to recover — which he almost immediately did.

The significance of Rasputin's influence over the czarina became apparent when World War I began, pitting the antiquated Russian army against the modern German war machine. The czar was persuaded to join his troops in the field, although he had no military competence; this left Alexandra in charge of the home front, with Rasputin as her main advisor. The imperial government was literally under his control. Under his direction, the czarina fired numerous experienced civil servants and replaced them with incompetents recommended by "Our Friend," as Rasputin was always called in the correspondence between the royal couple.

One of his appointees was nearly insane, others were little better, and all totally incompetent. If he had been a Bolshevik agent, he could not have done a better job in destroying the regime. Petitions poured in to the henpecked czar to do something about the situation. On the one occasion on which he tried to take a stand and refuse to approve the replacement of yet another official by a puppet of Rasputin, the czarina herself went secretly to his army camp to persuade him, and he caved in yet again. His wife always had two cards to play: she considered Rasputin a real man of God (since she was unaware of, or would not listen to, reports of his debaucheries), and the fact that only he had been able to help the crown prince when he was ill.

The "Friend" was finally assassinated in 1916, by men who saw no other way of dealing with him. They had a horrifying job of it, the bizarre details of which testify to the man's supernatural powers. The abnormal strength and resistance to death he displayed could well have been the result of diabolical possession. The conspirators' original plan was simply to poison the "monk," and on the advice of a physician, they laced some wine with enough deadly chemical to kill an elephant. Just to make sure, they put an equal amount in some cakes; Rasputin was known to be inordinately fond of both these delicacies. One of the conspirators then invited him to visit his home, an invitation which Rasputin eagerly accepted because he thought the man's wife would be there. He found that she had gone to visit her mother, and, making the best of things, he began to guzzle wine and eat cake, requesting that his host play the balalaika for him.

Soon it was clear that Rasputin had ingested enough of the poison to kill two elephants, but still he sat imbibing, as the young musician's nerve began to fail. Finally, when he saw Rasputin gazing knowingly at him, he realized his victim knew what was going on, and he fled the room. The conspirators in the other room told him he would have to shoot Rasputin, so he came back down the stairs with a pistol to find "Our Friend" looking at a curio cabinet with a crucifix on its top. "What do you think of that crucifix?" he asked. Rasputin did not care much for such things and gave a non-committal answer. "Grigori Ephemovich," said the other, "you had better look at that crucifix and say your prayers." Rasputin turned, was shot in the chest, at almost point blank range, and fell onto a white rug.

When the rattled plotters assembled to remove the body, however, not only was there no blood on the rug but the "corpse" reached out for the nearest throat, crying the man's name: "Felix! Felix!" Felix and friends fled in terror, and when they dared to return, Rasputin had managed to get out of the house and was crossing the court. Shot again, he was still not dead, so they bludgeoned him with a fire poker. They bound him tightly and threw him into the nearly frozen Neva River, but he still, apparently, was not quite dead, for when the body was recovered on the following morning, the ropes were found to be partially untied and the lungs filled with water — evidence of breathing.

He was gone at last, but the damage had been done. The administration was so destabilized that Marxist activists were able to take advantage of the bread riots of February 1917 to mount a revolution. The czar abdicated, almost without protest, and the "moderate" Communist Kerensky became head of the recently created parliament. Later that year, when the October Revolution occurred (in November according to our calendar), a more radical Communist regime rose to power, under the leadership of Lenin, Trotsky, and the young Josef Stalin.

A replay of the French Revolution
There are many eerie resemblances between the Russian Revolution and its French prototype: in both cases, a well-meaning but

indecisive ruler allowed things to slip from his control; both progressed in stages from initial acts of rebellion supported by moderate men to the extermination of the moderates and to mass atrocities; in both, the royal rulers were executed and the Church persecuted. Lenin himself was conscious of this connection with the French Revolution when he asked, "Where are we going to get our Fouquier-Tinville?" — a reference to the French revolutionary prosecutor who sent numerous victims to the guillotine. Echoing the Abbé Siéyès, Lenin declared, "Class enemies must be isolated, sent to concentration camps, in order to secure the Soviet republic."

Like the French revolutionaries, again, Lenin watched for an opportunity to destroy the (Russian) Church, and he found it when famine struck the Volga region. In a recently discovered letter to the Politburo in 1922, Lenin wrote, "Now, when there is cannibalism in the famine-stricken areas, we can carry out the expropriation of church valuables with the most furious and ruthless energy. . . . We must crush their resistance with such cruelty that they will not forget it for decades." And like some of the French bishops, such as Talleyrand, who cooperated with the French atheists, Russian Patriarch Tikhon stated in 1923, "I have completely adopted the Soviet platform."

Our Lady's messages and miracle

The child-seers of Fatima were aware of none of this, as they kept their monthly rendezvous with our Lady. In the first apparition, on May 13, 1917, the Blessed Virgin taught them a prayer, asked them to say the Rosary and to sacrifice for sinners, and to pray for the end of the war. In her second visit the following month, she announced that God wanted to establish on earth the devotion to the Immaculate Heart of Mary. The third apparition, in

July, included the famous vision of hell and the mysterious "Third Secret."

It also included a message that Sister Lucia was allowed to reveal only years later. In it, our Lady promised that the war was going to end, but that if men did not stop offending God,

> ... another and worse war will break out in the reign of Pius XI. When you see the night illumined by an unknown light, know that it is the great sign that God gives you that He is going to punish the world for its crimes by means of war, hunger, persecution of the Church and of the Holy Father. To forestall this, I shall come to ask the consecration of Russia to my Immaculate Heart and the Communion of Reparation on the first Saturdays. If they heed my request, Russia will be converted and there will be peace. If not, she shall spread her errors throughout the world, promoting wars and persecutions of the Church; the good will be martyred and the Holy Father will have much to suffer, various nations will be annihilated; in the end, my Immaculate Heart shall triumph. The Holy Father will consecrate Russia to me, which will be converted, and some time of peace will be given to the world.[8]

Our Lady further promised that in October she would tell the children her name and what she wanted, and would perform a miracle visible to all.

In the next two apparitions, the Blessed Mother repeated some of her earlier instructions, continued to urge prayer and penance, and mentioned again what she would do on October 13. On that day, she referred to herself as the Lady of the Rosary and promised that the war would end and the soldiers would soon be home. She also spoke again of how much our Lord was offended by sin and of the necessity for daily recitation of the Rosary and reformation of life.

Only the children saw our Lady that day (as well as a marvelous series of tableaux in which St. Joseph also appeared). But then, in full view of between 50,000 and 70,000 witnesses, pilgrims, and reporters gathered from all over Europe, the famous Miracle of the Sun took place. The sun seemed to spin in the sky, emitting colored rays, and then plunged toward the earth, terrifying the spectators, before returning to its normal place and state. People miles away reported seeing it — which rules out the claim of "mass hallucination" — and even the agnostic reporter of a socialist newspaper admitted to seeing the miracle, and he described it in detail. Thus did our Lady substantiate her message.

The horsemen of pestilence and famine

In the course of the twentieth century, all her prophecies would come true, one by one. World War I ended in 1918, the same year that the greatest influenza pandemic in history struck the world. It began in Kansas as a bird virus that had mutated, and was carried to Europe by American troops, where it apparently mutated again and became even more devastating. Some forty million people worldwide perished of the disease, sometimes within twenty-four hours. An unknown number also died of secondary infections or complications of the flu. Eighty-five percent of American war casualties were due to the influenza, not combat.

A decade after the end of the war, the Great Depression staggered the industrialized world with economic dislocation and misery. Unemployment and disruptions in the production and distribution of food led to famine in some parts of the world. During the 1930s, a man-made famine struck the Ukraine, where peasants had resisted both Communist control of their nation and collectivization of their farms. In one of the most chilling episodes in history, Stalin deliberately caused some five million peasants to be slowly starved to death by gradually confiscating their crops, food supplies, and anything else remotely edible.

Seven million Russian peasants who tried to resist collectivization were either shot or died in Stalin's slave labor camps, and tens of millions more would perish before the greatest mass murderer in history died himself in 1953. Yet the consecration of Russia to the Immaculate Heart of Mary, which our Lady explicitly requested on June 13, 1929, was not done. Pope Pius XI was informed of the events at Fatima and the messages of our Lady, but chose not to act upon them. This is somewhat puzzling, since it was during his reign (1922-1939) that the apparitions were investigated and approved. He was personally interested in them, and even distributed prayer cards with the image of Our Lady of Fatima. He was also acutely aware of the dangers facing the world, once stating, "Today we see something that world history has never seen before: the waving of the flag of Satan in the battle against God and religion, against all peoples, and in all parts of the world; a phenomenon that outdoes all that happened before."

Yet he did not make the consecration that our Lady promised would convert the unhappy country of Russia that must have been on his mind. Perhaps his many efforts to try to avert World War II preoccupied him; likely, too, his pursuit of the policy of conciliation with Bolshevik Russia begun by Benedict XV prevented him from doing what the Communists would see as a provocation. It's possible that Pius, like many leaders of the West (Solzhenitsyn wrote that in the period following the Revolution, "The Western powers bent over backward to prop up the economy of the Soviet regime") sought primarily to appease rather than upset the dangerous, unpredictable new Soviet Union.

War comes again

On the night of January 25, 1938, an extraordinary atmospheric phenomenon — a blood-red fire in the sky — lit up Western Europe. This puzzled astronomers; however, watching from her convent in Spain, Lucia recognized it as the promised sign that a new war was about to begin. Three months later, during the reign of Pius XI, Hitler annexed Austria, his first step in the series of conquests that would trigger the outbreak of world war the following year. Meanwhile, the Spanish Civil War had been raging since 1936, accompanied by a great persecution of the Church by anarchists and Communists. One-eighth of Spanish priests and numerous nuns perished, many gruesomely slaughtered. Only the victory of General Franco in 1939 restored order to the country and peace to the Church. He kept Spain out of the Second World War, but for much of the rest of the world, that war would be an unparalleled nightmare of suffering, ushering in both the atomic age and the Cold War.

Now, finally, our Lady was heeded in Rome, at least partially. In 1942 Pope Pius XII approved the reparatory devotion of the First Saturdays, and devotion to Our Lady of Fatima began to spread throughout the Church. Pope Pius did not, however, consecrate Russia to the Immaculate Heart of Mary, in union with the bishops of the world, as our Lady had not ceased to ask. He did make a consecration of the entire world, in October 1942, including a prayer for the conversion of Russia. Sister Lucia was told by our Lord that the days of the war would be shortened as a result of the pope's gesture, and in fact the turning point of World War II dates from that year: with the Allied victories at Midway, El-Alamein, and Stalingrad, the tide began to turn against the Axis powers. Still, the end of the war left Europe and much of Asia in shambles, and the Soviet Union in control of all of Eastern Europe. The

persecution of the Church under Communism, until its institutional collapse (at least in Europe) in the 1990s, caused untold suffering and death.

Is there a chastisement in our future?

We have seen, in our brief survey of a few episodes in Catholic
history, how failure to heed divine requests has sometimes been se-
verely punished. One sobering lesson might be drawn from the
Late Middle Ages, when the spiritual coldness and materialism
of which our Lord complained to his saints seem to have been
punished by the distressing climatic changes, famines, plague, and
wars of the fourteenth century. The paganism and worldliness of
the Renaissance period, combined with the ongoing craze for
money-making that would be such a prominent feature of modern
life, were accompanied by the Reformation heresies, devastating
religious wars, and the formidable onslaught of the Ottoman Turks
on Europe.

For a while, under the stimulus of the great Catholic Counter-
Reformation and the multitude of saints who promoted it, conversion and devotion seemed once more to flourish in the late
sixteenth and seventeenth centuries — at least in those countries
that remained faithful to Rome. But then came the Enlightenment, with its decay in morals at all levels of society and its sneer-
ing attacks on everything Catholic — from piety to politics. By
then, things had gone pretty far wrong, as we have seen in the previous chapter. Nevertheless, our good God, who never abandons
his flock, once again provided his people with a remedy: let the
king of France humble himself and make a solemn consecration of
himself and his country to the Sacred Heart, and all would be well.

As we have seen, Louis XIV refused. What need had he of divine help, when things were going so swimmingly for him already?

He would make a spectacle of himself if he performed such a novel consecration; he might look foolish. Worse, he might be expected actually to *practice* the new devotion to the Sacred Heart, like one of those "devout" ladies of his own court; who knew what that would do to his reputation? Better to skip the whole thing; no doubt this religious fad would blow over.

But perhaps that's not an apt comparison. Perhaps men are better now than they were in the seventeenth century, when our Lord complained of them to St. Margaret Mary. Perhaps we no longer deserve a chastisement like the French Revolution or need the consecration of Russia. Have men perhaps had a conversion, a change of heart, and now love God and avoid sin more than they did two hundred years ago? To ask the question is to answer it; one has only to look around. If anything, the world seems to have become yet colder to our Lord, and far more wicked in its ways than ever before in the Christian era.

Within the Church, the situation is no better. Today, in many of the old Catholic countries of Europe, something like five percent of Catholics — the people of Charlemagne and St. Odo, of Scanderbeg and Gregory VII — actually attend Mass regularly. Religious indifferentism, doctrinal confusion, and moral ambiguity have plagued the Church on many levels.

Such being the case, it might be a good idea to heed God's requests for prayer, penance, conversion of life, and yes, a special act of consecration of Russia by the pope and the bishops (although debate rages over whether this has already been fully accomplished; for my part, I think not). The Third Secret of Fatima, with its images of a ruined city, a chastising angel, and a crowd of martyrs that includes a pope, might be a glimpse into the consequences of continued disregard of its message. The historian cannot say, but can only point uneasily to what occurred the last time an explicit demand from heaven was ignored. Louis XVI made his consecration as an imprisoned king about to die, as his country descended into chaos and began to "spread its errors throughout the world." It came late — a hundred years late. We are not yet a hundred years from 1917, but we are getting there.

Could there be another "divine surprise"?

Here we come to the really consoling theme — which we can certainly use at this point in this book! If our Catholic past shows anything, it shows how God has often intervened just when things looked humanly hopeless, and turned history in a new direction: the conversion of Constantine comes to mind as but one example. Furthermore, we have actually been promised two great historical developments: the conversion of Russia (which Sister Lucia seems to have thought would be both rapid and complete), and a period of world peace. We have our Lord's word that these things will happen. This should give us great hope.

Just now we are living in the middle of an unfinished chapter, possibly the most interesting one — as well as the most perilous — in the whole history book of Christendom. It is, in fact, a great adventure, and one that could require of us high heroism and dedication. The message of Fatima includes requests not only for the popes and bishops for also for us, the faithful. The daily Rosary, the first-Saturday devotions, the prayers taught by St. Michael and by our Lady, and the penance of perfect fulfillment of the duties of our state in life are the weapons we of the Church Militant are to wield, motivated by our compassion and love for our Lord and our Lady, and our desire to make reparation.

We do not know when the day of peace will come, or what worse catastrophes might precede it. But the end of our real-life chapter will surely be a fascinating thing to experience.

To Learn More

What follows is not a bibliography of sources I used in writing this book. Many of those are scholarly works in languages other than English, and others are not readily accessible to the general reader. Instead, I am including a few suggestions for readers who would like to know more about some of the people and events covered in these pages. For them, there are two ways of finding more information:

• *Search online.* A Google search for a saint or another Catholic figure will generally bring up an excellent article from the early edition of the *Catholic Encyclopedia.* A search for primary texts from the Middle Ages will turn up *The Medieval Sourcebook,* a goldmine of letters, charters, historical accounts, and more related to medieval history.

• *Read a few books.* There are some excellent general histories of the Church readily available. For the earlier periods, I like the series by Henri Daniel-Rops. The English translation is excellent, the style is very readable, with dramatic incidents presented vividly, and it is rewarding either to read a volume all the way through or to pick out chapters at random. The first three volumes deal with material covered in our first four chapters: *The Church of the*

Ten Dates Every Catholic Should Know

Apostles and Martyrs; The Church in the Dark Ages; Cathedral and Crusade. These exist in several editions.

Much of what is written for the general reader about the Middle Ages is rot, and this is because of the anti-Catholic prejudices of so many modern writers. Two writers who can be trusted — and who have written some very appealing books — are Eleanor Shipley Duckett, author of numerous short works on the Dark Ages and interesting people who lived then, and Régine Pernoud, a French medievalist whose works on the High Middle Ages are starting to be translated and published by Ignatius Press. (*Those Terrible Ages* is one of them — a good antidote to the numerous worthless works on this glorious period.)

For the Protestant Revolution, Dr. Warren Carroll's *The Cleaving of Christendom* (Christendom Press) is a good recent summary. A brilliant survey by a non-Catholic that demolishes many of the myths of the Reformation and examines the essence of its success is *The European Reformation*, by Euan Cameron (Oxford University Press). Eamon Duffy's *The Stripping of the Altars — Traditional Religion in England c. 1400-c. 1580* (Yale University Press) provides an excellent view of the changes in the lives of ordinary people imposed by the English Reformation. There are more saints from this period and more biographies of them than could be listed here. In general, older works are more trustworthy and can be located through an Internet search.

For the wars against the Turks, Dr. Carroll's *The Cleaving of Christendom* discusses them as do most general histories. Googling "Lepanto" will turn up an excellent website devoted to that heroic battle, and there are Catholic biographies of St. John Capistrano, St. Pius V, and other heroes available online or in libraries.

For the French Revolution, it is a good idea to get a general overview and chronology from any history textbook (ignoring the ideology). Then read *The Guillotine and the Cross*, by Warren Carroll (Trinity Communications) and *Citizens — A Chronicle of the French Revolution*, by Simon Schama (Alfred A. Knopf). This is an example of "revisionist history" that dares to depict the Revolution as less than a glorious and beneficial event. It is a massive work, but well worth getting from the library and dipping into.

While the bloodbaths of the twentieth century defy summary, a few good short works exist on particular topics. Christendom Press has published Dr. Carroll's *The Last Crusade*, on the Spanish Civil War, and *Red Banners, White Mantle*, on the Russian Revolution. Both are excellent, as is his massive *The Rise and Fall of the Communist Revolution*. For Fatima, *The Whole Truth About Fatima* series (Immaculate Heart Publications) is a most readable and thorough study.

• *Novels*. Historical novels are often pure invention, but there are a few, written by Catholic scholars who knew their subjects thoroughly, that add considerably to our understanding of life in a particular period. For Christianity in Rome, two classics are Cardinal Wiseman's *Fabiola* and John Henry Newman's *Callista*. The second is more literary, but both are rousing stories. For the Reformation we are fortunate in having the several novels of Msgr. Robert Hugh Benson, convert son of an Anglican archbishop of Canterbury, who thus knew both sides of the distressing Reformation debate in England. His stories are page-turners, full of vivid characters, both historical and fictional. Listed chronologically from the reign of Henry VIII to the reign of Charles II, the novels include: *The King's Achievement; The Queen's Tragedy; Come Rack, Come Rope; By What Authority;* and *Oddsfish*. With the exception of *The Queen's Tragedy*, it is good to read them in chronological order because some characters appear in more than one book.

End Notes

1 Seneca, *Moral Epistles*.

2 Priscus, *De legationibus Romanorum ad gentes*.

3 Remigius, Letter to Clovis, 481.

4 Charlemagne, Letter to Abbot Baugulf of Fulda.

5 Cluny Foundation Charter, Duke William, 910.

6 Gregory VII, Letter to St. Hugh of Cluny, January 1075.

7 Frederick William Faber, *The Blessed Sacrament*.

8 Brother Michel de la Sainte Trinité, *The Whole Truth About Fatima*.

Biographical Note

Dr. Moczar is an adjunct professor of history at Northern Virginia Community College. She received a bachelor's degree in history and philosophy at San Francisco College for Women, and following two years' research in Paris, she obtained a master's degree at Columbia University. Her doctoral work was completed at Catholic University and George Mason University. She has written for *Triumph*, *Smithsonian*, *Catholic Digest*, *National Review*, and many other publications.

Sophia Institute

Sophia Institute is a nonprofit institution that seeks to nurture the spiritual, moral, and cultural life of souls and to spread the Gospel of Christ in conformity with the authentic teachings of the Roman Catholic Church.

Sophia Institute Press fulfills this mission by offering translations, reprints, and new publications that afford readers a rich source of the enduring wisdom of mankind.

Sophia Institute also operates two popular online Catholic resources: CrisisMagazine.com and CatholicExchange.com.

Crisis Magazine provides insightful cultural analysis that arms readers with the arguments necessary for navigating the ideological and theological minefields of the day. *Catholic Exchange* provides world news from a Catholic perspective as well as daily devotionals and articles that will help you to grow in holiness and live a life consistent with the teachings of the Church.

In 2013, Sophia Institute launched Sophia Institute for Teachers to renew and rebuild Catholic culture through service to Catholic education. With the goal of nurturing the spiritual, moral, and cultural life of souls, and an abiding respect for the role and work of teachers, we strive to provide materials and programs that are at once enlightening to the mind and ennobling to the heart; faithful and complete, as well as useful and practical.

Sophia Institute gratefully recognizes the Solidarity Association for preserving and encouraging the growth of our apostolate over the course of many years. Without their generous and timely support, this book would not be in your hands.

www.SophiaInstitute.com
www.CatholicExchange.com
www.CrisisMagazine.com
www.SophiaInstituteforTeachers.org

Sophia Institute Press® is a registered trademark of Sophia Institute. Sophia Institute is a tax-exempt institution as defined by the Internal Revenue Code, Section 501(c)(3). Tax I.D. 22-2548708.